A SIAMESE EMBASSY
LOST IN AFRICA 1686
THE ODYSSEY OF OK-KHUN CHAMNAN

BY

MICHAEL SMITHIES

SILKWORM BOOKS

Other books edited by Michael Smithies
in the Treasures from the Past series

A Resounding Failure: Martin and the French in Siam 1672–1693
Chaumont and Choisy: Aspects of the Embassy to Siam 1685
The Siamese Memoirs of Count Claude de Forbin 1685–1688
Alexander Hamilton: A Scottish Sea Captain in Southeast Asia 1689–1723
Pierre Loti: A Pilgrimage to Angkor

***

ISBN 974-7100-95-9

First published in 1999 by
Silkworm Books
54/1 Sridonchai Road, Chiang Mai 50100, Thailand
E-mail: silkworm@pobox.com
Website: www.silkwormbooks.com

Set in 11 pt. Garamond by Silk Type
Front cover: Ok-khun Chamnan Chaichong drawn by Carlo Maratta
(BAV, Vat. Lat. 14166).
End papers: View of the Bay of Good Hope from Guy Tachard, *Voyage de Siam, 1686*

Printed by O.S. Printing House, Bangkok

CONTENTS

CONTENTS

LIST OF ILLUSTRATIONS

Rome, Vatican Library, BAV. Vat. Lat. 14166
[Reproduced, with permission, from *Twenty-five Years*
***of Thai-Vatican Relations* 1994]**

PREFACE

This long-forgotten tale of the shipwreck off the coasts of Africa of a Siamese embassy to Lisbon in 1686 lies buried in the text of a French book that has not been printed since 1689. The author of the text was the intrepid and intriguing Jesuit Tachard, who published accounts of his first two journeys to Siam. In his second book, written when Tachard was King Narai's personal envoy to Louis XIV and Pope Innocent XI, he relates the account of the shipwreck as told by one of its survivors, Ok-khun Chamnan Chaichong, who was accompanying Tachard on his return to France.

Ok-khun Chamnan during his odyssey as part of the aborted embassy to Portugal spent nearly a year in Goa, where he learnt Portuguese, a month travelling overland from Cape Agulhas, the southernmost tip of Africa, to the Cape of Good Hope, four months at the Dutch settlement at the Cape, six months in Batavia, and several months at sea on this journey. On his return to Siam in 1687 he was ordered to greet the French envoys La Loubère and Céberet soon after their arrival.

The adventures of this Siamese *khunnang* did not end with his unsuccessful journey to Lisbon. He went on to Europe in 1688, visited the Riviera and Rome in winter, met the pope, and then in 1689 had an audience with Louis XIV. He converted to Catholicism and returned from Europe in 1690, disembarking at Balassor in Bengal before returning via Mergui overland to Ayutthaya.

The fascinating and improbable account appears in English here for the first time, accompanied by supporting texts of Choisy, Tachard, and La Loubère describing the Dutch settlement at the Cape, with several contemporary prints.

Tachard was not famous for his exactitude, as the postscript here shows, but contemporary Dutch sources prove that he did not invent the story of Ok-khun Chamnan's African adventures. He was though clearly guilty of putting some of his own thoughts and reactions into Chamnan's utterances, as the notes show.

The short text nevertheless has its moments and its interest. It would make a marvellous film, full of action and adventure. The film rights have been retained.

My thanks go to all those who have helped in preparing this book, notably to Dr. Dhiravat na Pombejra, whose checking in VOC archives verified Tachard's account of Ok-khun Chamnan's travails.

Michael Smithies
Bua Yai
April 1998

INTRODUCTION

King Narai of Siam (reigned 1656–1688) practised, as a counterbalance to growing Dutch influence in the region, a policy of opening to the world, and in particular, from 1680, sought French support. From 1683 he was increasingly under the influence of his favourite, the Levantine Constantine Phaulkon (Ok-ya Wichayen), a convert to Catholicism and considered by the French, for whom he was 'Monsieur Constance', as chief minister, though he appears to have been the *phra klang*, in effect the minister of foreign affairs and trade, without taking the title. The last three years of Narai's reign saw a continual exchange of embassies with the French, though the second French mission to Siam in 1687 was more an expeditionary force, with secret orders to seize Bangkok and Mergui if they were not handed over voluntarily to French troops.

The first Siamese embassy to Louis XIV and the pope, which left Ayutthaya in 1680, ended in disaster, with the ship carrying the mission wrecked in a storm off Madagascar towards the end of 1681, with no survivors. The king's follow-up mission of 1684 at least arrived, via London, and met the French monarch, but the envoys were ill-formed, uncouth, and compared by their Missionary interpreter, Bénigne Vachet, to buffaloes. It had one important consequence: Vachet, on very slender grounds, persuaded the king's confessor, the Jesuit Fr de La Chaize, and

1

through him the king, that if a sufficiently important embassy were sent to Siam, its king might convert to Catholicism.

This led to the sending of the first French embassy to Siam, headed by the Chevalier de Chaumont and with the Abbé de Choisy as co-adjutant ambassador. Needless to say, it failed to convert King Narai; it also failed to obtain satisfactory terms of trade, its other objective. It returned to France in 1686 with the Siamese embassy led by Kosa Pan, which was a huge social success.

But the Siamese embassy was excluded from negotiations which went on behind its back between the court and the Jesuit Guy Tachard. Tachard had gone to Siam for the first time with the 1685 embassy with the intention of proceeding with five others to China, but had then become involved in Siamese affairs through his close association with and support for the plans of 'Monsieur Constance'. Phaulkon, foreseeing the demise of his patron, King Narai, and anxious to secure his own position, probably through a pliant successor, proposed settling French-men in key positions in the country, and the handing over of the port of Songkhla or some other place.

He was more than disconcerted when the Siamese embassy returned with the La Loubère-Céberet mission of 1687, accom-panied by several hundred troops, and demands for the surrender to French forces of Bangkok, 'the key of the kingdom', and the port of Mergui on the Andaman Sea. Tachard also accompanied the mission, with secret instructions to deal directly with Phaulkon, making impossible the position of the envoys extraor-dinary, the more so as Tachard only followed Phaulkon's will. Apart from trade concessions prised out by Céberet, the diplo-matic mission accomplished little, and La Loubère left Phaulkon on the worst of terms, with French troops precariously en-trenched in Bangkok and about to leave for Mergui. They were ousted from these places in 1688 after the murder of Phaulkon, the death of Narai, and the accession of Petracha to the throne, when Kosa Pan became *phra klang*, minister of foreign affairs and trade.

Although La Loubère and Céberet were sent as envoys extraordinary and not ambassadors, with the hopes that the distinction would be appreciated in Siam and their mission would not result in a return Siamese embassy (as Lanier remarks, the constant exchange of envoys and presents was beginning to fatigue the French court), King Narai determined on sending a further mission to France, which would also call on the pope, Innocent XI. As we have seen, the first Siamese embassy to France was also due to have gone to Rome with letters and presents from Narai but never reached its destination. The king decided, probably at Phaulkon's urging, to send Fr Tachard as Siamese envoy on a second embassy to Rome, though he was not given the title of either ambassador or envoy extraordinary because of his cloth. To give the mission a Siamese flavour, though, three 'mandarins' were selected to accompany the Jesuit; in the words of Tachard, "Three mandarins embarked on the squadron to accompany the letters of the king" (1689: 301).

Tachard, in his hastily compiled account of his *Second Voyage . . . au Royaume de Siam* (1689)—it was put together using texts drawn from various sources, with plenty of typographical mistakes, and even serious errors in the pagination—thinks so little of these three that neither in the published version of his voyage, nor in his unpublished *Relation*, which is largely a justification of his actions in relation to Phaulkon and a virulent attack on the principal French envoy extraordinary, La Loubère, does he even bother to give the names of any except one, and then only his first name.

The three were Ok-khun Chamnan Chaichong, Ok-khun Wiset Puban, and Ok-muen Pipith Raja, though the records are not clear which of these was the most senior. We know more about Chamnan, who had apparently been selected to take part in an earlier embassy to Portugal which left for Goa at the end of March 1684, arriving more than five months later. As the Portuguese fleet had left for Lisbon, the embassy spent nearly eleven months in Goa waiting for a ship to take it to the Portuguese capital. The embassy embarked at Goa on 27 January 1686, but the Portuguese vessel was shipwrecked on 27 April off Cape Agulhas, the southernmost tip of Africa; Chamnan and his surviving companions had to undertake the difficult journey overland, which lasted thirty-one days, before reaching the Dutch outpost at the Cape of Good Hope. From there, after spending four months recovering and waiting for a ship, he went to Batavia in Java, spending six months there again waiting for transport, and returned to Siam in September 1687, without ever having reached his destination.

During his travels to Goa, the Cape, and Batavia, Chamnan managed to pick up some Portuguese, the *lingua franca* then in use in Southeast Asia for communication with Europeans, which Tachard thought an advantage, and is advanced as a reason why Chamnan was selected to participate in the 1688 mission. But he had already been pressed into court service before his departure. Tachard's version of Chamnan's travels includes his meeting the French envoys La Loubère and Céberet soon after their arrival at the Bar of Siam, on 4 October 1687. Céberet left a record of that meeting:

> The 4th, two *ok-khun* from the palace came on board from the king to pay us compliments. We learnt subsequently that these were much more important people by their standing and their rank, which is, nevertheless, of some consideration. They were both well turned and much more polite and witty than is common among people of this nationality. We received them in Mr de La Loubère's cabin which is more commodious for such an occasion. We were seated in armchairs, placed at the end of the room on a carpet, on which there were cushions for the mandarins. They sent first their interpreter, who was Portuguese, as they spoke not French, to ask if we were able to receive them, and we told them they came most opportunely; having received our reply, they came and, on entering the room, left their slippers at the door, and gave their greeting, which is to bring the two hands together in front of their face. They seated themselves on the cushions, their interpreter remaining standing behind

them. They remained silent in the manner of Orientals who never speak first out of repect. We asked them news of the king's health, to which they replied, and then paid us compliments on behalf of their master about our arrival, telling us of the joy this had given him and all his subjects. The rest passed in compliments and civilities on both sides concerning the union and friendship of the two kings. After that tea was served in the fashion of the Indies, and then they withdrew onto their galley where they wrote down the smallest details to give an account of what had taken place. (Jacq-Hergoualc'h 1992: 56)

The new mission, with the French Jesuit Tachard representing the Siamese king to Louis XIV and the pope, left Siam on the *Gaillard* on 3 January 1688 with the returning envoy extraordinary, La Loubère (Céberet had gone overland to Mergui and then separately by ship from Pondichéry). The journey was fraught, as the emnity between La Loubère and Tachard was now open, and Tachard sank into paranoia, even accusing La Loubère of cutting a hole in the partition separating their cabins so that he could read Tachard's documents. Their ship reached Brest on 25 July 1688, and Tachard went ahead to give his report to the court at Versailles, leaving his mandarins to their own devices. They re-embarked at Brest, went to Rouen with the presents from their king and Phaulkon, and reached Paris on 14 September, with three catechists from Tonkin and five Siamese schoolboys selected by King Narai to pursue their studies in the college of Louis-le-Grand following on the 17th.

The French king was at Fontainebleau and, undoubtedly aware of the conflicting accounts of La Loubère, Céberet, Forbin, and Tachard concerning the limited value of Siamese trade, the little likelihood of the conversion of King Narai, and perhaps concerned about the position of his troops in Bangkok in Mergui, deferred the planned audience in December with the latest emissaries, and decided the Siamese and Tachard should go to Rome first. As Tachard hoped to leave France and return to Siam in

March 1689 with yet another French expedition, he made all haste to leave for Rome.

Accompanied by his three mandarins and two of their valets, Tachard left Paris on 5 November 1688. Their interpreter, Moriset (sometimes Morisot, and Tachard's erstwhile assistant and secretary) went on ahead with two other Siamese valets, the bales of presents, and three Tonkinese catechists who were going to Rome as representatives of the Christians in their country seeking the reinstatement of the Jesuits there. Tachard's party went first to Lyons by stage-coach, and then the whole group went down the Rhone as far as Avignon. There they took litters as far as Cannes, where they arrived on 26 November 1688.

From Cannes they took two feluccas, first to Villefranche, then to Monaco, "to show our health papers", where unfavourable weather made them stop and allowed for some sightseeing. They then continued along the Côte d'Azure and the Italian Riveira, taking in San Remo and Savona before arriving in Genoa on 2 December, where they spent two days. From Genoa, they travelled at first overland, then again by sea, to Rapallo and Sestri Levante, arriving in Livorno (Leghorn) about 7 December, where they spent a week. They left Livorno on 16 December, after being well entertained there, and, proceeding by boat, passed Piombino, and Porto-Hercole, to reach Civitavecchia, the port for Rome, on 20 December. Tachard went overland from there to Rome, while the mandarins went up the Tiber to the eternal city on 21 December.

The secretary of the Propagation of the Faith, Cardinal Cibo, sent one of his coaches to take the mandarins into the city; the French Cardinal d'Estrées also sent horses to greet them, as did the pope's majordomo, Mgr Visconti. They were lodged in a villa next to the Jesuit College, wined and dined, and given Swiss guards to protect them.

The mandarins were granted two sumptuous papal audiences. The first took place on 23 December 1688, with Tachard acting throughout as envoy, with the *khunnang's* presence being largely decorative; it was Tachard who addressed the pope and who presented the letters and presents from King Narai and Phaulkon. The Siamese were dispensed from kissing the papal feet. At their farewell audience on 5 January 1689 they were assembled with the Tonkinese catechists, and received medals from the pope's hands; they had earlier been given "packets of preserves, divers medals and boxes of fragrances . . . and each Siamese valet was given three silver medals" (Tachard 1689: 415).

Whilst in Rome, they visited the Basilica of St Peter and other renowned churches, the Sistine Chapel, the church of the Gesù, the city's fountains, the palaces of the pope's nephew, the Duke of Ceri, Livio Odescalchi, and the Prince and Princess Borghese, and of course the papal palace in the Vatican, where they admired the library, its arsenal, the Belvedere gardens and climbed into the dome of St Peter's. The Vatican resident artist, Carlo Maratta (1625–1713), whose painting of the Virgin and Child, "decked with a precious frame", was given by the pope to Tachard to take to Phaulkon, made sketches of the three mandarins, bearing their names in Siamese characters, and which are preserved in the Vatican Library; these are the only known illustrations of the mandarins.

The *khunnang* left Rome on 7 January, arriving at Civitavecchia the following day, where they were received by the governor at the head of the garrison. On the 9th, Tachard embarked with the three mandarins on two well-armed Maltese ships for Marseilles.

The French court circular, the *Mercure Galant,* of March 1689 gave details of the journey of the Siamese mandarins to Rome in the company of the Tonkinese catechists and Fr Tachard, the information apparently coming from Tachard's *Second Voyage,* and mentioned the fact that Louis XIV granted them an audience, but did not describe the event or give the date. It must have taken place in February, on the 25th of which month Tachard, as the envoy of King Narai, ratified in the presence of Louis XIV the treaty of commerce Céberet had obtained in 1687. Tachard signed on 1 March a further document concerning relations between the two countries. Two weeks later Tachard signed in the name of the King of Siam a treaty with the Marquis d'Eragny, who had been appointed to the post of captain of the palace guard in Ayutthaya as well as inspector-general of French troops in Siam.

But political events in Europe checked even Tachard's Siamese ambitions. The War of the Grand Alliance (1689–1697) broke out, bringing France into conflict with the League of Augsburg, including the Austrian emperor, Sweden, Spain, and some German princes, joined by the Netherlands, Savoy, and England. French ships were needed closer to home, and, as the season for sailing to Asia passed, reinforcements for Siam were deferred until 1690.

The three mandarins were stranded in France, but little is known about their activities while Tachard was busy signing treaties for Siam at the court. Unlike the ambassadors of 1686–7, those in the capital in 1689 caused little comment. The two memorialists of the period, Dagneau and Sourches, made no mention of their presentation at court or of their subsequent doings. Then came news of the revolution in Siam via the prisons of Middelburg in which French captives, taken at the Cape on returning from Siam, were incarcerated. Dagneau in his memoirs speaks of the news of the revolution in Siam on 5 November 1689, and Sourches of the "events" in Siam on 6 November 1689. The *Mercure Galant* of November and December 1689 also gave news of the revolution in Siam and French prisoners interned in Holland.

The news reached Tachard when he was at Saumur; the departure of French ships for Siam was again deferred. Tachard was in Port-Louis on 18 November, probably arranging for the shipment of goods to Siam on French Company vessels; it is known, from Challe, that the three mandarins spent some time in Port-Louis, though the dates are uncertain. Tachard in November broke the news of the revolution in Siam to his three tame mandarins, then in Brest, presumably waiting there for the departure of French Navy ships. They were not excessively disturbed, and held that Narai was a harsh and feared ruler; the sister of one of the mandarins was married to the nephew of the new king; Petracha's son was thought by them capable and fond of mathematics. By this stage all three had been sufficiently exposed to Catholicism and were baptised in the Jesuit church in Brest. They were apparently holed up in Brest until the departure of the Duquesne-Guiton fleet of six ships on 25 February 1690 for Siam, which it never reached.

One of the three *khunnang*, Ok-muen Pipith, had the misfortune to die on board the *Gaillard* on 10 March, and was given a six gun salute as an "honour appropriate to the first Siamese mandarin to die a Christian." (Vongsuravatana 1992: 157). He died off Cape Verde, probably from the excessive heat, rather than from a marked addiction, like his colleagues, to French wine, which Challe (1979: 61) had noted.

The squadron anchored at the Cape Verde and the Comoros islands, and Pondichéry. There, the director of the French East Indies Company, François Martin, noted in August 1690 "The Rev. Fr Tachard and M. Charmos embarked on the squadron in the hope that M. Duquesne gave them of reaching Mergui. Fr Tachard only took with him the Siamese who were returning from France." (Martin 1934: III, 113). The squadron continued to Balassor, near the mouth of the Ganges, but, because of unfavourable winds, never reached the Siamese port of Mergui; instead, it hung around the Negrides for weeks while the crews died in large numbers of tropical diseases and scurvy. When battles took place, Tachard "prudently remained with the two mandarins at the bottom of the hold" (Lanier 1883: 183). Finally Mergui was abandoned as a destination in favour of returning to Balassor. Ok-khun Wiset and Ok-khun Chamnan were offloaded at Balassor between 4 and 30 December, when the *Gaillard* with the rest of the Duquesne-Guiton squadron docked to take on supplies and land their many sick; the Siamese were given a five gun French salute as they left to take "a Moorish vessel", according to Lanier (1883: 183). Martin, writing in January 1691, is less specific: "The Rev Fr Tachard left at

Balassor the Siamese he had brought from France for them to travel to Mergui or Siam [Ayutthaya] when the first chance arose." (Martin 1934: III 137). Challe, citing Martin, said they took either a Dutch or a Portuguese ship to Mergui (Challe 1979: 442–3), instead of leaving them in Pondichéry to take a French vessel back to Siam.

From the Siamese port they travelled overland to Ayutthaya, bearing a grovelling letter from Tachard to the new *phra klang*, Kosa Pan. There is some indication in Martin's *Mémoires* that the Siamese might have thought the French, or possibly just Tachard, were keeping the two remaining mandarins as hostages. The Siamese sent early in 1691 as envoy to Pondichéry Vincent Pinheiro, "a native of Siam but a Christian, who had been interpreter for the gentlemen of the [French] mission and then of the [French Indies] Company", who had been raised in rank to that of Ok-luang Worowathi for his mission and given two deputies and some valets. Writing in January or February 1691, Martin noted:

> He has been sent on the return to Siam by the persons of that nation whom Fr Tachard had left in Bengal and who had afterwards returned from there. These persons [Ok-khun Chamnan Chaichong and Ok-khun Wiset Puban] had been given a letter for the *barcalon* which the Rev. Fr Tachard had written . . . The envoys were charged with the *barcalon's* reply for His Reverence. (Martin 1934: III, 184)

The reply was not favourable; Tachard was clearly informed he would not be welcome in Siam.

Thereafter Ok-khun Chamnan and his companion pass out of history. It is not known if they abjured Catholicism on their return, or if they met Tachard in January 1699 when the court at Ayutthaya finally condescended to receive the Jesuit, who presented a ten-year-old letter from Louis XIV addressed to Phra Narai, dead for nearly eleven years, and a letter from Pope Innocent XI, similarly addressed, and who had died ten years earlier.

But Narai not only sent embassies to France and Rome, and it is from Tachard's published account of the second French mission to Siam that we learn of another embassy he sent to Portugal in 1684. The account of this fills most of Book VII of his *Second Voyage* (1689: 309–375). This, as will be seen, was no more successful in reaching its destination than Narai's first embassy sent to France, but at least there were some survivors.

Tachard introduces this digression to his text as his returning ship, the *Gaillard,* approached the Cape of Good Hope.

> The sight of Cape Agulhas [Needle Cape] recalled to Ok-khun Chamnan ['Occum Chamnam'], one of the mandarins whom I brought with me, the shipwreck he was involved in a few years before, on board a Portuguese vessel, which was lost, and the details of which adventure I felt obliged to ask, which he often said was one of the most extraordinary which had ever arrived to any traveller. I found it such indeed, and wrote it down as he related it to me. I present it here with great pleasure as all the details which the mandarin gave me were found to agree with the testimony which some Portuguese, whose word can be relied on, had given me and who were his companions on that voyage, and who took part in his adventure. Those who have seen him in Paris, where he remains [March 1689], will have no difficulty in believing all his story, and the reflections he made during this account, which is given in entirety, almost word for word as he related it to me. (1689: 309)

Ok-khun Chamnan's account, as related by Tachard, follows. The sub-headings have been added, and the original terms in the text, 'Hottentots' and 'Kaffirs', retained; they acquired, like 'negroes' and 'natives', their politically incorrect overtones in more recent times.

The Dutch fort at the Cape of Good Hope

PART ONE

THE ODYSSEY OF OK-KHUN CHAMNAN

THE JOURNEY TO GOA

The King of Portugal[1] had sent to the king our master a very important embassy, either to renew their old alliance or to negotiate other secret matters about which I was unaware. To return the civility of this European monarch, the king named three important mandarins as his ambassadors,[2] with six other young mandarins, accompanied by a fairly large retinue, to go to the Portuguese court. We embarked for Goa towards the end of March 1684 on a frigate belonging to the king our master, commanded by a Portuguese captain. The voyage was long, difficult, and full of misadventures, which seemed to anticipate the ill-success of our journey, and the misfortune which would befall us. We spent more than five months making this journey, although Goa is not far from Siam. Finally, either the officers and the pilots were incompetent, or the weather being set against us, the Portuguese fleet had left the Indies before we arrived in this capital city of the Portuguese empire in the Orient. It was a very serious inconvenience for us to see our departure from the Indies, and consequently our return to Siam, delayed without recourse for a whole year, but we had to be patient.

1. Pedro II, regent from 1667, king 1683–1706.
2. It was the Siamese custom to send three ambassadors, the *ratchathut*, *uppathut*, and *tritut*, in descending order of rank and usually age, on each overseas mission.

We stayed nearly eleven months in Goa, waiting for the return of the Portuguese fleet which was due from Europe, bringing the king's orders to permit us to leave that year on vessels destined for Lisbon. Such an extended period did not seem to be long, because we used our time very agreeably. The novelty and beauty of the buildings which we saw in that city surprised me considerably; the great number of palaces, monasteries, and churches, all so rich and sumptuous, filled our curiosity for a long time. As I had never left my country before, I confess I was surprised to see that there existed in the world a city finer than Siam.[3] The viceroy had us lodged magnificently, and desired to defray, on behalf of the King of Portugal, all our expenses during our stay, though he was somewhat annoyed that the king our master had not sent a letter to him.[4]

After such a long stay, we finally embarked for Europe on a vessel belonging to the King of Portugal with a crew of a hundred and fifty men and some thirty cannons. There were many passengers who were going to Portugal, for in addition to the ambassadors, with numerous persons in their retinue, and three priests belonging to different orders, namely a Franciscan, an Augustinian, and a Jesuit, there were in addition many Creoles, Indians, Portuguese, and half-castes who were making the journey.

---

3. Ayutthaya.

4. This situation was to be repeated in reverse soon after. François Martin, in his *Mémoires*, wrote from Surat in March 1685: "An envoy from the viceroy of Goa had arrived in Siam with a letter to the King of Siam complaining about the French bishops and Missionaries, even requesting him to oblige them to leave the kingdom, because of falsely reported insults which they had given to the Portuguese priests and monks. The King of Siam, who was better informed, paid no attention to this. The envoy was not received with the distinction he expected, because he brought no letter from the King of Portugal. The court at Siam nevertheless resolved to send envoys to Goa when the viceroy's envoy returned" (Martin 1932: II, 383).

SHIPWRECK OFF CAPE AGULHAS

We set sail from the roads of Goa the 27th of January in the year 1686,[5] and the 27th of April at about midnight we unfortunately ran aground on Cape Agulhas[6] in this manner. The same day at sunset several sailors had been sent to climb the masts and yards to reconnoitre the land which we could then see a little to the right before us, and which had been in sight for three days previously. Following the reports of the sailors, and other indications, the captain and the pilot judged that it was the Cape of Good Hope which we were approaching. So, without checking themselves to see if the sailors' reports were true, and without taking any other precautions, they continued their course until two or three hours after sundown, when they thought they had passed the land which had been seen. Then changing direction, they shifted slightly to the north. As the weather was clear, there was a fine moon, and a strong fresh wind, and it was said with assurance that we had passed the Cape; the captain put no one on guard on the lateen yards. The watch sailors were indeed on the look-out, but it was for manoeuvres or to chat together, with so much confidence in themselves that no one saw the danger that lay before us, and did not even believe it was possible for there to be any until it was too late to avoid it. I was the first who saw land.

I do not know what foreboding of misfortune overhanging us made me so unsettled that night, but I could not close my eyes to

5. Chamnan/Tachard's dates do not accord with the length of time he gives for his journey to and stay in Goa. If he left Siam in March 1684 and took more than five months to get there, the embassy arrived about August 1684. The Siamese spent nearly eleven months in Goa, meaning they left Goa about July 1685, not 27 January 1686. One does not know whether to believe the dates or the stated periods of time; both are likely to be wrong. Chamnan is not likely to have used a Western calendar, and his memory may be at fault for the number of months passed at sea or at Goa.

6. Cape Agulhas (Needle Cape), the southernmost tip of Africa, is some 180 km as the crow flies from modern Cape Town, which grew from the Dutch settlement founded in 1652.

sleep. Not knowing what to do, I left my cabin and occupied myself in watching the ship which seemed to glide over the water. Looking a little ahead, I suddenly saw on our right a dark shadow close to us. This sight frightened me, and I at once asked the pilot, who kept watch at the tiller, if it was not land which I saw ahead. As he came up to see for himself, the cry went up from the prow of the vessel, "Land, land ahoy; we are done for; hard to starboard." The pilot pushed the tiller to change course, but we were so close to the shore that, in tacking, the ship hit a rock three times on the stern, which caused it to foul its direction. These three blows were very strong, and we thought that the vessel had broken up. The pumps were manned, but at that point no water had come on board. This gave some heart to the crew, which thought its time had come when the ship first hit the rock with so much violence.

As soon as it was seen that water was not being shipped, steps were taken to get out of this untoward situation by cutting the masts and making the vessel lighter; but there was little time, because the waves, pushed by the winds towards the shore, carried the ship with them on mountains of water which broke on the shoals that advanced into the sea, raising the ship to the skies, and then letting it suddenly fall on the rocks with so much force and speed that it could not survive intact for long. On all sides it could be heard breaking up. The spars came away one after the other, and this huge wooden mass could be seen to shake, fold, and give way everywhere with a frightening noise and crashing.

As the poop of the vessel was the first to strike land, it was also the first to give way. Well might the masts be hacked off, cannons thrown into the sea, along with chests and everything met with in this disorder, to relieve the vessel by making it lighter; all these precautions and efforts were to no purpose. The shoals were hit so often and so roughly that it finally split beneath the powder magazine. Water came on board in abundance, and began to reach the first deck, filling the powder magazine. It even reached the main cabin, and soon was waist-high on the second deck.

At the sight of this a great cry went up, and everyone went to the highest point of the boat in such confusion and so suddenly that several, in their haste to save their lives, ran the risk of losing them. The powder magazine and the first deck being full of water, all the ship's biscuit, brandy, and wine at the bottom of the hold were lost, and we were unable to take advantage of them. The water still slowly rising, our ship gradually sank into the sea until the keel touched bottom, when the hull remained for a time immobile.

It would be difficult to describe the fear and consternation which then afflicted everyone, and I am not capable of describing the scene. Who can say or even imagine what thoughts the perspective of a certain and frightful death gives rise to? Only cries, shouts, and sobbing could be heard. People bumped into each other; those who had been the worst enemies became sincerely reconciled without constraint; some were on their knees or prostrate on the deck imploring the assistance of God; others threw barrels into the sea, empty chests, masts, yards, and other large wooden objects to escape on them. The noise and tumult were so horrible that neither the din of the ship as it broke into a thousand parts nor the sound of the waves as they broke on the rocks with incredible fury could be heard.

After this lamentation had passed, those who still remained on board thought of saving themselves. Several rafts made from planks and ship's masts were devised, because the first people to jump into the sea did so thoughtlessly and either drowned, or were crushed by the violence of the waves which threw them on the rocks strung along the shore.

It was a sad and tragic sight indeed to see so many poor people in such peril and without any likelihood of aid. I was at the time as astonished and frightened as the others at first; but as I was assured that it was possible to save oneself, and seeing that I lost little in this shipwreck, I consoled myself and decided at once on my course of action. I put on the two suits of clothes I possessed which were quite clean, and then, getting on some planks of wood that were tied together, I tried to swim to the shore. The second ambassador, the strongest of the three, and the best swimmer, was already in the water. He went ahead of me, and carried the king's letter[7] tied to a sabre which His Majesty had presented to him. Thus both of us reached the shore almost at the same time. Several Portuguese had already arrived there, but they were no less concerned on land than those who remained on the ship. The former saw that they were indeed out of danger of drowning, and the latter still faced this. But it seemed that the former had escaped this great peril only to succumb to another still more terrible and certain. They had neither water, wine, nor ship's biscuit; they did not even know where these could be found. Moreover the cold on land was very penetrating, and we were the more sensible of it as we were not used to it. Seeing that I was very lightly clad, I realized that I could not long survive thus. This made me decide to return the following day to the vessel to look for clothes and seek out victuals. Most of the more important Portuguese had their cabins on the first deck and I decided that I would find there objects of great value, and in particular a good supply of provisions which were in our extremity the most needed. For the rigours of the cold, the exhaustion of the night, hunger, and the little likelihood of finding water or victuals, made our condition almost as unfortunate as that of those whom we had seen disappear and drown before our eyes. With these thoughts I got abreast a kind of wattle, and swam to the vessel.

I had little trouble in boarding it, because, as I have already said, it was still above the waterline. I thought I would find gold and precious stones, perhaps a valuable commodity which would be neither too cumbersome nor too difficult to carry off. But on arriving I saw that all the cabins were full of water, and I could only remove some lengths of gold stuff, a small cellaret with six flasks of wine, and a little ship's biscuit, which I found in a pilot's cabin. I tied all these things together on the wattle I had brought along, and pushing them ahead with much difficulty

---

7. The Siamese treated a king's letter with as much reverence as the king himself. More is made of this letter later by the second ambassador.

and danger, I once again reached the shore much more exhausted than on the first occasion.

There were some Siamese who had managed to escape but were entirely naked. In the compassion I had of their misery, seeing them shaking with cold, I gave them the cloth I had brought from the ship, which they wrapped around them at once. But I clearly saw that if I gave them the cellaret of wine which I had brought, it would not last long in their hands. I gave it to a Portuguese who had shown himself very friendly towards me, saying that I made him master of it, as long as he gave me some when I was in need. On this occasion I quickly learnt how much friendship is weak when faced with necessity, and how little one is concerned by the needs of others when one is oneself in want. This friend gave me a half-glass of wine to drink each day for the first two or three days, while we hoped to find at any moment a spring or a stream. But when pressed by thirst, and almost no fresh water was found to assuage it, I tried in vain to get him to share what I had confided to him out of sincere friendship; he rebuffed me so roundly the first time, saying he would not even give some to his father, that I did not dare ask him again. As for bread, there was none, because everything was soaked in sea water, and I never could digest any, so bitter and salty was it. When it was clear that no more people would come ashore, the number of those who had been saved was counted, and came to almost two hundred persons; so that there were only seven or eight drowned who had been too precipitous in trying to save themselves. Some Portuguese had taken the precaution of bringing with them muskets and powder, either to defend themselves against the Kaffirs, or to kill game, so as to have something to eat in the forests. These muskets were of great use to us in making fire, not only during our long journey to the Dutch outpost, but above all the first two nights when we were cast on the shore all dripping in sea water; for the cold was then so biting that if a fire had not been lit to dry our garments I think we would all have died of cold in that place.

Zebras or wild donkeys at the Cape

THE TREK BEGINS

The second day after our shipwreck, a Sunday, the Portuguese having said their prayers, we all set off together. The pilots and the captain told us that we were not further than twenty leagues[8] from the Cape of Good Hope, where the Dutch had a considerable settlement, and that only one or two days were needed to reach it. This assurance they gave us meant that many left the victuals they had brought from the ship to be less encumbered and to cover more quickly and easily the little stretch which remained to be travelled.

We entered the forest, or rather the bush, for there were no large trees, and we hardly saw any throughout all our journey. We walked the whole day, only stopping two times to rest a little. As we brought nothing to drink nor eat, we began to feel the first attacks of hunger and thirst. Our thirst was especially intolerable, for we walked under the sun's rays with great diligence in the hope of arriving that day at the Dutch settlement. About four in the afternoon we came to a great pool which was a considerable relief to everyone. Each of us drank his fill, with such relish and pleasure that none had experienced until then. The Portuguese were of the opinion of not continuing and to remain the oncoming night beside this pool. A fire was lit, and those who found some crabs in the water roasted and ate them. The others, in greater number, after drinking a second time, went off to sleep, much more fatigued by the long stage of the journey than oppressed by the hunger which tormented them during the two days they had not eaten.

The following day we left when the sun was up, after each of us had drunk to hold at bay the thirst which would be encountered. The Portuguese went ahead, since we were obliged to stop because of the first ambassador who was very weak and listless, and unable to hurry. But as we should not lose sight of the Portuguese, we split up into three groups. The first always kept the

8. About 80 km; a league is approximately 4 km.

21

last of the Portuguese in sight, and the two others walked the same distance behind, following signs which the first group had left as agreed, to give warning of when the Portuguese stopped or changed course. We came to some low mountains which did not fail to exhaust us as we were obliged to climb over them. On the way, we only found a source with water so brackish that no one was able to drink it. We saw at the same time that those in the first group left a sign that the Portuguese had stopped; we did not doubt that there was some good water there, and this hope made us quicken our pace. However, whatever efforts we made, we could not bring along the first ambassador except in the evening after sundown. Our men told us that the Portuguese did not want to wait for us, saying that we gained nothing by dying with them of hunger, thirst, and in need; that it was much better for them to go ahead and look for some food for us.

The first ambassador, on learning this sad news, called together all the Siamese who remained with him, for there were three who still followed the Portuguese. Seeing us all around him, he said that he felt so weak and exhausted that it was impossible for him to follow the Portuguese, and he considered it appropriate that those who were in good health should hurry to catch them up; he only instructed them that since the Dutch dwellings were not too far off to send him a horse or a cart with some provisions to transport him to the Cape if he were still alive. This separation was very sad for us, but necessary. There was only one young man, aged about fifteen years, the son of a mandarin, who refused to abandon the ambassador, who loved him dearly, and whom he held in great affection. His gratitude and affection made him decide to die, or else to save him, together with an old servant who likewise remained with his master.

The second ambassador, another mandarin, and myself, having taken leave of him with the assurance of bringing him help as soon as possible, set off, intending to catch up with the Portuguese, although they were far ahead of us. The signs which the Siamese furthest ahead had left on top of a mountain with their banner increased our courage and made us redouble our steps.

However, as fast as we travelled, we did not arrive close to them on this high mountain before ten in the evening. We thought there would be water to drink in that spot, and we would be able to rest for what remained of the night; but we were sadly disappointed in our hopes. After rejoining the Siamese, they told us that the Portuguese were still encamped not far from there, and showed us the fire they had made. Howsoever exhausted we were, we had to proceed, and after two full hours of travelling through woods and rocks, we arrived there, with incredible difficulty. They were posted on the outcrop of a high mountain, where they had lit a big fire around which they had fallen asleep. Each of us asked where the water was found. One of my friends brought me some, for the stream which had been found was quite far from there, and it would have been impossible for me to drag myself there. I stretched out flat on the ground, by the fire, unable to move; sleep overcame me in this position, until the morning when the cold woke me up.

That day I felt so weak, and was racked by so cruel a hunger that I wished to die a thousand times over. I resolved to stay where I was, and wait for death, since it was pointless to seek it out further ahead accompanied by fresh torments.

This thought did not remain long with me, and when I saw the Portuguese and the Siamese who, though as dejected as myself, still continued their journey to guarantee their lives, I could not resist following them. I even went ahead of them once, reaching the summit of a hill, where I found extremely high grass in great quantity. The haste I had made greatly fatigued me, and I was obliged to lay down a little to one side on this fine greenery, where I fell asleep. When I woke up, I felt my thighs and legs so stiff that I thought I had lost the use of them. This dire situation made me return to my thoughts of the morning. I was so resolved that I waited for death with impatience, as a moment to finish with all the unfortunate ills which overwhelmed me on all sides. I fell asleep with this thought, and without the intervention of a mandarin who was my special friend, and my valet, who had sought me out for a long time,

Hottentots, inhabitants of the Cape

thinking I had lost my way, and who having found me woke me up, I would for certain have died at that spot. The mandarin said so many encouraging things to me that I took heart; I got up, and we went together to find the Portuguese who were stationed next to a mountain torrent. Our hunger was so extreme that they set fire to the grass in the places where it was partly dried, to flush out some lizards or snakes to eat. One of the group found some leaves at the water's edge and tasted them; though they were very bitter, after eating some he felt his hunger assuaged. He came to give the good news to the whole company. Everyone ran off in a hurry and avidly ate them. Thus did we spend the night.

FIRST ENCOUNTER WITH HOTTENTOTS

The following day was the fifth of our march; we set off in the morning, secure in the thought of finding Dutch dwellings that day. This flattering conceit gave us new strength. We walked without stopping until midday, when we saw some people on a hilltop quite far off from us. We did not doubt but that they were the persons we sought. We walked towards them with unimaginable joy. But this comforting thought did not last long, and we were soon sadly disillusioned. The people we had seen were three or four Hottentots who, having spotted us first, came up to face us with their lances, or rather their assegais, and inspect us. Their fear, on seeing so large a group which was armed with muskets, was no less than ours. For our part, we were terrified, seeing us about to be mercilessly massacred by these barbarians. As they came to us with their assegais and were only four or five, we thought they had come to reconnoitre us, and that their companions would not be far behind. We let them approach, persuaded that it was better to finish this life for good than to prolong it and lose it in the end after suffering a thousand torments more cruel than death itself. But when they saw us closer, though still some way off, and observed that we were much more numerous than they had first imagined, they stopped, and waited for us in their turn. We came up to them in extreme incertitude; but as soon as we had somewhat approached them, they took the initiative, and made signs to us to follow them, indicating some dwellings, that is three or four miserable huts perched on a hill. When we reached the foot of this hill, they refused to let us get closer to their huts. There was a small path along which they led us to another village, ever looking at us mistrustfully, and observing our progress. When we had arrived at this village numbering some forty or so huts covered with branches of trees, and perhaps containing four or five hundred persons, they then showed some assurance, and boldly came up to us, looking over us at leisure. They took particular pleasure in looking at the Siamese in the party, either because our clothes pleased them, or because, having never seen anything like us, they took pleasure in satisfying themselves with our novelty. Their curiosity became irksome to us, and all of us wanted to enter their huts in search of something to eat; for, in spite of the signs we made that we were extremely hungry and wanted them to give us food, they looked at each other, and began to laugh very heartily, without appearing to understand us.

When we requested of them by signs as best as we were able to sell us some of their numerous cattle or sheep which we could see feeding in the surrounding countryside, they only spoke two words, which they repeated all the time, "Tobacco, patacas".[9] I offered them two big diamonds which the first ambassador had given me when we left him; but they took no heed of them. None of us had any tobacco, or any patacas, which were the only currencies they understood and which were used among them. The first pilot alone had some with him; he gave them four for a bull which they usually only sell to the Dutch for its length in

9. The pataca was a silver coin used in Portuguese, Spanish, and also it would seem Dutch settlements, and remains the name of the currency of Macao. In the seventeenth century it was also known as a piece of eight, a dollar, or a patacoon, and was worth about four shillings and eight pence.

tobacco; but what was that among so many people half-dead with hunger, who had only eaten a few leaves for six whole days? The pilot only shared his prize among a few of his fellow-countrymen and his best friends. No Siamese could taste a single sliver. So we had the cruel vexation of seeing ourselves die of hunger in the midst of abundance, without being able to touch it; for the Portuguese also forbade us to approach the Hottentot herds with the intention of seizing some cattle as much as they prevented us from partaking of the bull they had cooked, saying that if they saw we seized a cow or a sheep, they would abandon us to the fury of these barbarians.

A mandarin, seeing that the Hottentots did not want any minted gold, put some gold ornaments on his head, and showed himself to them. This novelty pleased them, and they gave him a quarter of mutton for these objects, which were worth a hundred pistoles. But to what does necessity reduce us! Nothing can withstand hunger, especially when it is so excessive. This meat could not be cooked quickly enough; we ate it half-raw, and it only served to give us an appetite. I noticed that the Portuguese, after buying their bull, had skinned it, and had thrown away the skin. This was a treasure for me. I told a friend, the mandarin of whom I have spoken, about this in confidence. We went to seek it out together, and happily found it; we then put it over the fire to cook it. It only lasted us two meals, because the other Siamese, having noticed us, had to be given some. A Hottentot, after looking very closely at me, was fascinated by the gold buttons I had on my dress. I gave him to understand that if he wanted to give me something to eat, I would willingly give them to him. He agreed, and went off to find something for me. I expected to have a sheep at least, but he only brought a bowlful of milk, and I had to be content with that.

We spent the night in that place, close to a big fire lit in front of the Hottentots' huts. These barbarians did nothing but shout and dance around their dwellings until day broke, which put us on our guard for fear of being surprised, for there can be no doubting it, that if they were able to dispose of us, they would have done so at whatever cost. We left there in the morning, and set off in the direction of the shore, which we reached at midday. It was a delight for us to find mussels there, all along the coast. After having eaten our fill, we collected some for the evening, for it was necessary to re-enter the woods to look for water. As much as we searched, we did not find any until nightfall, and it was only a thin trickle of water, and very dirty at that; but at that point we did not have the leisure to let it settle before drinking it. We camped by this small stream, and each kept guard in turn during the night, for fear those Kaffirs might come and attack us with the intention of massacring us. We maintained this habit of keeping watch at night in turn, and shouting out from time to time, to show that we were not asleep, and were on guard.

THE ISLAND OF DELIGHTS

The following day, the ninth of our trek, we came to the bottom of a high mountain which could only be traversed with extraordinary difficulty. Hunger attacked us more mercilessly than ever, and we found nothing to assuage it. From the top of the mountain, we saw on a flank some quite attractive grasses and also some flowers. We ran to that spot and began to eat the least bitter with a voracious appetite. But in assuaging the hunger which beset us, our thirst increased and caused us torments inconceivable to anyone who has not been in such an extremity. However great was our burning thirst, we had to wait until evening before being able to drink, as we found no spring or stream until well into the night at the foot of this steep mountain. We could not pass around it, and it was there that we held counsel, and it was agreed by all not to continue inland as we had done to shorten our route, firstly because the captain and the pilots confessed they were mistaken, not being able to disguise their error any more, and they added that they were uncertain of the place where the Dutch were to be found, and the route one should take and the time needed to reach them; secondly because by staying close to the sea, we would find mussels, crabs, and other creatures more easily than inland, and with these the cruel torments caused by hunger could be assuaged; and that finally the rivers, streams, and springs all ended in the sea, so that by walking along its coasts we should not suffer excessively from thirst.

To implement this decision taken the previous evening, as soon as it was daylight we took the direction of the sea coast. We arrived there two hours before midday. We first saw a broad beach with at its extremity a vast mountain advancing far into the sea.[10] This sight pleased everyone, because the pilots assured us it was the Cape of Good Hope. Such good news gave us strength, and without taking rest, we set off to reach it before night fell; and though some five or six leagues had to be covered, we walked with so much strength and courage, notwithstanding our extreme fatigue, that we arrived there an hour before the sun set at the foot of this vast cape we had seen in the morning. But by mishap it was not that which we had been led to hope. After having given over to the vexation of seeing ourselves still so far off our destination, and almost without hope of arriving at the Dutch dwellings, we consoled ourselves with the words of a sailor, who had gone off scouting the terrain, who told us that nearby was a small island almost entirely covered with mussels, and with a strong spring of fresh water. We decided to spend the night there, but we found ourselves so satisfied with the good refreshments found there, that we stayed there the whole of the following day, and the following night too. This stay rested us considerably, and the food we ate there allowed some of our strength to return. The first evening, on arriving, we gathered together as was our custom a little apart from the Portuguese, and were very surprised not to see one of our mandarins any more. We looked for him everywhere, and called out to him, but in vain; he had stopped on the wayside, lacking the strength to continue. The great aversion he had to eating grass and flowers, which all the others ate with but little relish, did not allow him

10. This was possibly the promontary known now as Danger Point.

Rhinoceros

even to bring them to his mouth. Because of this, we were not surprised that, having stayed so long without eating anything, he died of hunger and weakness, without being capable of calling out, and without being seen by anyone. We had lost another in the same fashion four days before. Want must indeed harden the heart. In any other condition than that in which I found myself, if I had learnt that one of my friends had died in such a pitiful fashion, I would have been inconsolable; but, then, the sentiment I had over the loss of this mandarin, whom I knew very well, hardly affected me. All we did was to express some regrets at his death for a moment, and each then went his own way to find something to eat.

THE PANGS OF THIRST AND HUNGER

After staying two nights and one day on this island which I have already spoken about, we set off for the Cape. Before leaving, we had noticed some dry and fairly large trees, open at both ends like trumpets. Thirst, which until then had seemed so cruel to us, inspired us to adapt these in a way that proved very useful. Each of us took one of these long tubes, and having tightly closed it at the bottom, we filled it with water to last the whole day. Given the uncertainty of the location of the Cape of Good Hope, the pilots said it would be a good thing to climb a high mountain in front of us, because perhaps from the summit we might have some certain indication of the place we were seeking. No more was needed to persuade us all. We climbed this very steep eminence as best we could, and had to do so with extreme care and make extraordinary efforts to cross it that day, going to the right where the mountain was not so high and abrupt. Throughout the whole of that day we only lived off some small flowers and a little greenery which we found here and there in small quantities. Coming down this mountain in the evening, with much regret at not having found what we sought, we saw a herd of elephants half a league ahead of us, grazing in a broad open plain. There must have been twenty in all, not one of them very big. We spent the night by the shore at the foot of this mountain. The sun had not yet set when we arrived at the place where we were to encamp. We spread out on all sides, everyone seeking something to eat; but we found nothing on the shore nor inland.

Of all the Siamese, I was the only one to find something on which to sup. I sought out grasses, or some flowers to eat, but only found those so bitter that they were impossible to swallow. After having for a long time uselessly employed myself thus, I noticed on returning what was in truth a very thin but fairly long snake. It was not thicker than my thumb, but was fully as long as my arm. I followed it as it tried to escape, and killed it with a blow from my dagger. We put it on the fire with no other preparation, and ate it whole, with its skin, its head, and its bones, without anything being left over. It seemed to us very tasty, and I never encountered any meat better than that throughout all this journey. After this light supper, we regretted the absence of one of our three interpreters. He was destined to go to France with two mandarins who were to carry to his Most Christian Majesty a present from the king our master; and so only ten Siamese remained, including the two ambassadors.[11]

We broke camp that day rather later than usual. At dawn, a thick fog came up which obscured the whole horizon, so it was already broad daylight when we set off. Hardly had we covered a quarter of a league, when a very unpleasant wind blew up, the strongest I have ever experienced in my life; and apart from it being excessively cold, and coming straight at us, it was so violent that we were unable to put one foot before the other. Perhaps, given the weakness of our condition, we thought the wind stronger than it really was. Whatever the case, we were obliged to tack, as they say at sea, and change our course, that is, we went

11. The interpreter had apparently either fallen by the wayside or died. It may seem unlikely that King Narai would send via Goa and Lisbon an envoy with a present to Louis XIV, as he sent envoys in 1684 and 1686 by other routes, but his desire (or that of Phaulkon) to establish close contact with the French court was strong, and Lisbon was an established transit point.

first to the left and then to the right to move ahead. About two after midday the wind brought on a drenching rain which lasted until evening. It was so heavy and dense that we could only seek shelter from it. Some did so under some dried-up trees, others went to hide in the hollows of rocks, and several, finding no other place to shelter, stood with their backs against the escarpment of a ravine, and stayed close to each other to get some warmth, and endure with the least inconvenience the violence of the storm. It would be difficult to make others understand the distress and pain we endured from the cold, the wind, and the rain for the rest of the day, and all the following night. We counted for nothing the extreme hunger which racked us, having found nothing to eat during our trek, and having only drunk the rain which fell. The lassitude and other fatigues of the preceeding days seemed tolerable in comparison to the misery and the ills we then suffered, continually trembling and thoroughly drenched through without being able to close our eyes, or even to lay down and rest a little.

THE PORTUGUESE ABANDON US

Never had a night appeared so long, nor so tiresome, and it seemed we were relieved of half our troubles when we saw the dawn break. Our torpor, weakness, and other afflictions can be imagined after spending such a dreadful night. But we Siamese were still more surprised, and certainly more saddened, when, getting ourselves ready to join the Portuguese, we saw they were no longer there. We looked all around, cried out to them and searched everywhere; it was not only impossible to find a single one of them, but even to know the route they had taken. So cruelly abandoned, all the misfortunes we had suffered until then returned to overwhelm us and make us feel them the more. Hunger, thirst, weakness, sorrow, fear, fury, and despair took possession of our hearts. Only half-alive, we looked at each other in surprise, in total silence, devoid of feelings. Then, somewhat rallying from that condition, the second ambassador was the first to take heart, and tried to rouse the others. He called us together to consider what we were going to do in the present situation, and spoke these words to us:

"You see as well as I do, faithful Siamese," he said to us, "the unfortunate state to which we are now reduced. After the shipwreck we suffered, in which we lost everything, there still remained some consolation. While we remained with the Portuguese, they acted as our guides and in some respects as our protectors, be it against the fury of the elephants, tigers, lions, and other beasts of these vast forests, or against the the inhabitants of these lands, who are still more cruel and more to be feared than the fiercest animals. I would like to believe that, having treated us so well up to now, they have but left us for very particular reasons.

"Have we not had to abandon our first ambassador in horrible solitude, with the intention of bringing help to him, if we are lucky enough to be able to do so? In the loss of two of our mandarins, and other Siamese who have so far died, we have learnt that, in extreme necessity, one has few feelings of sympathy for the misfortune of one's kin, and that, through privations oneself, and seeing others suffer, one has no pity left for anyone. So I do not blame their decision, which may be praiseworthy. We must only blame our fate which caused us to be separated from them this night, and which has prevented us from learning the direction they took. But even if they abandoned us without reason, it is not the moment to complain about them. In blaming their cowardice, and their lack of concern for us, we do not overcome the great dangers which assail us. Let us try to forget them, in order not to have the cruel displeasure of remembering that they abandoned us, or that we have lost them; and let us act for now as though we never knew them. We have, in truth, received from them some slight relief, but we can suffice without it. Perhaps God, who governs heaven and earth,[12] touched by the merits of

---

12. This is an unlikely comment from a Siamese Buddhist, and is certainly an intrusion of Tachard into Chamnan's account.

our great king, seeing us destitute of all human aid, will take particular care of our destinies. So, without further ado, we have but to follow the seashore as we had previously decided.

"There is but one thing which we can prefer above all others and about which, if I were certain, I would not concern myself with my fate, howsoever unfortunate it might be. You are all witnesses to the profound respect which I have always shown for the letter of the great king our master. My first, my unique concern in the shipwreck, was to save it. I can only attribute my salvation to the good fortune which always accompanies one who once had the honour to approach the supreme majesty of the great king whom we serve. From the time of the shipwreck you have seen with what concern I carried the letter. When we camped on the mountains, I always took care to place it in the topmost position, or above the head of those in our group; and, while placing myself lower than it, I still remained at a suitable distance to protect it; and when we stopped in the plains, I always placed it at the top of the highest trees which I could find near us. When travelling, I carried it on my shoulders as long as I could, and I have never assigned it to anyone else, except when my strength was almost beyond lifting myself. In the uncertainty in which I find myself, if I cannot follow you much longer, I order, on behalf of the king our master, the third ambassador [to carry it]; he will take care of it, and if he succumbs after me, to act likewise with the first mandarin, and in the same circumstances; I order, say I, the third ambassador, if I die before him, to take the same care of this august letter, so that, not being able to carry it to the person to whom it was destined, as long as a Siamese remains, may one of you place it in the hands of His Majesty. And if, in the worst of outcomes, none of us succeeds in reaching the Cape of Good Hope, he who is the last to be charged with carrying it shall bury it, before dying, on a mountain, if possible, or in the highest point which can be found; and having placed this precious relic in safety from attack or accident, he may die prostrate beside it, showing after his death the respect that was its

Stag at the Cape

due during his life. This is what I have to say to you. After this injunction, let us resume our courage, let us never separate from each other, and travel in short stages; the benevolence of the great king our master will ever protect us, and the stars which oversee his happiness will see to our preservation."

This speech made a great impression on our spirits. We were all fired with vigour, and resolved to carry out his orders. We agreed we had to follow the Portuguese as best we could, and to follow the path which we thought was the one they had taken. So, without tarrying further, we set off. Before us lay a fairly broad and high mountain, and a little to the right a low hill. Seeing the steep sides of the mountain, we readily concluded that the Portuguese, tired as they were, would not have had the strength to climb it. It seemed to be the most direct route, but as it was impossible to take it, we judged it best to move to the right and travel over the eminence which we saw in front of us. That day, after the unfortunate night we had spent, brought me strange pains, not just because of my stiff and numbed legs, but above all because they started to swell up, along with my whole body, in an extraordinary fashion. A few days afterwards, a whitish frothy puss started to come from my body and especially from my legs, causing me terrible pains which lasted throughout the voyage. Without having experienced this, I could never have imagined that a man's life was sufficiently strong to resist for so long such a terrible multitude of violent agonies.

THE GREAT RIVER

We were travelling fairly quickly; at least, it seemed as though we were moving speedily, though in fact we did not cover much ground. About midday we arrived very wearily and much fatigued at the banks of a river which was some sixty feet wide, and seven or eight feet deep. When we reached the bank, we doubted that the Portuguese had crossed it, for, though it was not particularly wide, it was extremely swift. We tried to cross it, but the current was so rapid that it would have carried us off if we had not retraced out steps very quickly.

However, in our uncertainty as to whether the Portuguese had passed beyond that point, we resolved to try to cross it once more. To do so with less danger, we tried a stratagem which, however, did not work. We tied together all the scarves we possessed, deciding that the strongest among us would travel across, carrying one end of our line which he would tie to a tree to be seen on the opposite bank, and so that everyone, thanks to this long scarf, would be able to travel to the other bank without being carried off by the strength of the river. The most muscular mandarin in the group was charged with this task, but he was only in the middle of the river when the strength of its current was such that he let go of the end of the scarf, and only reached the other bank after almost succumbing to the waters. The river flowed with such force that in spite of all his efforts, and using all his skill, he was thrown against a spit of land projecting into the stream; his shoulder was badly bruised and his body battered. He went on foot alongside the river, opposite us, and shouted that it was impossible for the Portuguese to have taken this route. We told him to return to our side, but to do this he had to travel a long way upstream from us, before swimming across, and he still had trouble in climbing the bank where we waited for him.

Being persuaded that the Portuguese had not crossed the river, we concluded that they must have travelled upstream alongside its bank. We took this route, after refreshing ourselves with some water, though we found nothing the whole day to eat. We had but covered a half a league when we found a stocking, all torn, which convinced us that Portuguese had taken this route. After many difficulties, we reached the base of a mountain which had a hollow at its foot, as if nature wished to offer a shelter to passers-by. There was enough room for us all to shelter there, and we spent a very cold and consequently very unpleasant night there. For some days my feet and legs were so swollen that I could neither wear stockings nor shoes;[13] but this disadvantage was made much worse by the extreme cold I suffered that night, and the humidity of the rock face. On waking in the morning I discovered the patch of earth under me covered with water and puss which had oozed from my feet. However, though I was very weak, I found enough strength that day when the others were preparing to leave. It seemed as though the more I suffered, the more I clung to my life, as though it had become more precious, having become more miserable, though I hoped more than ever to save it, after having suffered so long and so cruelly, and run so many risks of losing it.

DEATH AND CONFUSION

We continued alongside this river bank the following day in the hope of finding the Portuguese, whom we thought not far off. From time to time we found traces of their passage. At a quarter of a league from the rock where we spent the night, one of our people found, a little to one side, a flintlock with a full powder horn, which a Portuguese had undoubtedly abandoned, having no more strength to carry them. This find was of great use to us subsequently. We removed the butt and the barrel, and took the striking mechanism with the powder horn to make a fire. This came very opportunely, for since we followed the course of this river, we had found nothing [to eat], and were almost dead from hunger. We immediately lit a fire, and seeing that my shoes were not only useless, I not being able to wear them, but were in addition cumbersome, having to carry them in

---

13. Like the wine mentioned as being unavailable after the shipwreck, this lack of shoes and stockings seems culturally inappropriate. Either Chamnan had become very westernized in his eleven-month stay in Goa, or else Tachard is intruding his own imaginative views here. One of the few striking things in Chaumont's account of his embassy in 1685 was his frequent reference to the Siamese mandarins being without shoes and stockings.

my hands in the hope that my swellings would subside, necessity overrode any other consideration. I tore them apart, and after grilling them at length, we ate them with much gusto. We did not find them very tasty, for the leather was so dry that not a drop of juice remained in them; but it was enough that they were not bitter, and could be swallowed, so great was the hunger that tormented us then. We then tried to eat the hat of one of our valets, after cooking it over the fire for some time; but we could not succeed in digesting it. To be able to chew it, the pieces had to be cooked to a cinder, and were then so bitter and so disgusting, that our stomachs rebelled, howsoever raveneous we might be.

After this meal, we resumed our journey, and we noticed again when going up a hill a clear indication that the Portuguese had followed the course of the river like us. This was one of our interpreters who had followed them, whom we found dead, his knees on the ground, and his hands, head, and the rest of his body slouched over. The two interpreters who had still survived, being half-castes, that is with both Portuguese and Siamese parents, had not wished to be separated from the Portuguese, and had abandoned us the day they left us, in order to join them. This one appeared to have died of cold, seeing him slumped over his knees, propped against the hillside, at a spot entirely covered in grass. We stayed a while in this place which seemed very pleasant, with its fine wholesome greenery. Each of us gathered a small supply of the least bitter grasses and leaves to form our supper that evening.

We followed our path which began to seem very tiresome, seeing that the Portuguese were ever in front of us, and we were exhausting ourselves spending so many days without being able to catch them up. There was not one of us who was not angered at having come so far with so much difficulty. We regretted especially the small island we had passed three or four days before, where we had found good fresh water, and a quantity of mussels, which had formed the best food we had eaten throughout our journey.

Discord and vexation increased that evening. When we arrived at the place where we intended to sleep, there were but two possible paths to follow, both very difficult, and it was impossible to know which of the two the Portuguese had taken. On one side there was a very steep mountain, and on the other a fen crossed with numerous watercourses made by the river which we had followed, and which in many places flooded part of the countryside.

We could not believe that the Portuguese had crossed the mountain, up which it was necessary to climb a lot; it was still more difficult to know if they had entered the marshes which appeared almost completely flooded, and where we could see no trace of them, nor any sign which caused us to suspect they had passed that way.

In this dilemma we discussed for some time into the night the course we should take, if we should continue, or if we should retrace our steps. The difficulties lay in deciding which route to take had so greatly alarmed us that everyone was agreed not to continue, especially when one considered the impossibility of traversing the fen without running the risk of a thousand deaths; and if we crossed over the mountain, we ran the risk of dying of hunger and thirst, because there was no sign of water there, and a day or two would be spent in crossing it.

PROSPECTS OF SLAVERY

After coming to this resolution, we all agreed to return to the islet which I spoke about just now; we would stay there three or four days, living off mussels found there in plenty, waiting for news of the Portuguese; and after finishing these victuals, if no help came, we would go and seek out the Hottentots in the forest, and offer ourselves to them as herdsmen, and serve them as slaves. This condition seemed infinitely more desirable that the wretched state to which we had been reduced for so long.

We hoped that these people, howsoever barbarous they were, would be touched by our distress, and the work we would do for them would require them to give us some food so that we did not die of hunger at their hands. This last formulation to which our misery reduced us shows the deplorable state to which we had been brought. One really has to be destitute to think oneself happy to serve as a lackey the most abject, filthy, and abominable people on earth, whom one would not wish to receive in one's own home even as a slave.

Having taken this decision, we waited for dawn before setting off. As soon as day broke, we departed, and walked with so much courage in the hopes of finding once more this idyllic isle, and to relieve there our hunger which became every day more intolerable, that we reached it in three days. As soon as we found this delightful spot, which was so salutary for us, we felt an extraordinary joy. Each of us tried to reach it first, but the speed of the most impatient was to no avail, for the tide cut off its approach. This isle, to speak more precisely, is only a fairly high circular rock, perhaps a hundred paces round at high tide, and when the tide was out, small rocks could be seen all around on the strand. There was a sandy path which linked the rock to the mainland, which could only be crossed when the tide was out. As the tides when we were there were high, they covered the path which led there with more than five feet of water. We spent five whole days there, going there when the tide allowed, looking for mussels which remained on the sand between the rocks. After collecting enough for the day, we ate some, and spread the rest out in the sun, or cooked them for the evening. All the nearby coasts were deserted and so arid that we could only find a few shrivelled bushes to make our fire, which we could not do without. For hardly had we fallen asleep at night, than we woke, all stiff and numb with cold.

Seeing that wood was lacking on the shore, some of us went to look for it inland, but thereabouts were only treeless sandy deserts and abrupt rocks, with no greenery. A lot of elephant dung was found, which was used for two or three days to keep our small fire going. When this last resource failed, the intensity of the cold caused us to abandon this island which had supplied us with victuals in such a timely fashion in our moment of dire need, and we set off to look for the Hottentots. Our vexation was increased by the sad thought that we were going to serve under and be dependent on the most repulsive and barbarian people in the universe. But what would we not have done to preserve our lives which had cost us so dearly up to then, in the hopes of improving our condition?

After spending six nights there we left our mussels and fresh water with much regret. What decided us to depart from this place was that, since we had no news of the Portuguese, we thought that they had either all died en route, or that they thought we in turn had died, or that the people they might have sent to look for us would not find us on this remote island.

Before setting off, we took a supply of fresh water and mussels; each of us took as much as he could carry. We went to sleep the first day on the shores of a salt pan, quite close to a mountain where we had previously camped. It was a good thing that we had taken a supply of fresh water and mussels for the whole day, for we found nothing which could be eaten. As soon as it was light [the next day], each of us went in search of food and water. We hunted all around for grasses or leaves; we still had our mussels, but we wanted to set them aside for a more pressing necessity. Some of us went into the lake to look for fish, but to no purpose, for it was just salt water with a muddy base.

HOTTENTOTS AGAIN

While everyone was thus scattered, those near the lake saw three Hottentots who came up on their right. Immediately, one of our group gave a signal, and we all gathered together as we had previously agreed, and waited for these three Kaffirs who walked with great strides to reach us. As soon as they came up to us, we knew that they were in touch with Europeans by the pipes they smoked. At first we were in as much difficulty as them for making ourselves understood, for when they were close to us, they made hand gestures, extending six fingers, and shouting as loudly

Sea cow

as they could, "Hollanda, Hollanda!" They indicated with their fingers the path we should take, and gave signs for us to follow them. At first we were unsure what to do. Some of us thought that these three Hottentots were spies, emissaries of those we had previously met, and who wanted to massacre us. Others thought that their signals meant that the Cape of Good Hope was only six days' walk ahead. We discussed these possibilities some time, and decided to follow these guides wherever they led us, for nothing worse could happen to us than what we had already experienced, and death itself would only end our distress which had made life itself so cruel and so troublesome. We were not long in holding to our first suspicions that these Hottentots were spies, and we soon recognized that they were not so primitive as the first lot we had met, and had had contact with Europeans. They had brought with them a quarter of mutton; hunger made us ask for it, but they gave us to understand that we could have it only if we gave them some money. After indicating that we had none, they showed us that we should give them our gold and silver buttons. I gave them six gold ones, and they handed over the quarter of mutton which I immediately grilled and then shared out among those of our party.

As soon as they had met us, these Kaffirs strongly urged us to follow them, and did all they could to get us to move on and hurry our pace. They went ahead of us, and after walking for a time, returned to us to urge us on. It was about midday when we left the salt water lake and these Hottentots brought us to camp close to a slight eminence. We rested at the base of this, though the Hottentots, who were far from being as weak and exhausted as us, called us to join them at the summit, and spend the night there. The path was very rough, and we walked a great deal. Of the fifteen of us who remained, seven were so exhausted that they were unable to put one foot in front of the other, when it came to walking the next day.

We held counsel about what to do in this sad extremity, and resolved to leave there the weakest with some of the dried mussels which we still had, assuring them that as soon as we had found a Dutch settlement, we would send them comfortable carriages. Howsoever painful this separation, they had to agree to it, since they were completely incapable of continuing. In truth, we were all in a very bad state. There was not one among us who did not have his body, and especially his thighs and feet, extraordinarily swollen; but the poor Siamese we left behind made us afraid for them, so hideous and distorted were they. We who set off were greatly distressed at leaving our comrades, not being sure of ever seeing them again; but they would have received no succour from us if we had stayed with them to die alongside them. After bidding them a sad farewell, those among us who were not so enfeebled set off following our guides, who had woken us very early in the morning.

As I was one of the first who was ready to leave, I witnessed something rather disagreeable to see and talk about, but which should be known to appreciate the filth and stench of this revolting and unspeakable tribe. After our three Hottentots had made a fire in the morning to warm themselves, the night having been very cold, seeing that we were ready to depart, they took the dead embers, and after putting them in a hole they dug for the purpose, they urinated on them, and pounded the mess together for some time. When the result was fairly liquid, they rubbed it all over their bodies, their arms, legs and faces for some time. After this fine ceremony, they presented themselves to us. They were very impatient with our slow pace, but nothing could be done about it. Finally, they tired of us, and after speaking to each other for a while, two of them raced ahead with great speed. The third remained ever with us, never leaving us once, stopping when we desired and as many times as we needed to do so.

We spent six whole days following our guide with such difficulty, and we were so exhausted that they seemed much more intolerable than all the previous days. We had always to climb and travel down such frightful places that just looking at them made us afraid.

Even this Hottentot, hardened throughout his life to climbing the rudest heights, had trouble in mastering this rough terrain.

Some of us decided to attack him, seeing him beginning to climb such a steep mountain that they thought it impossible to pass, persuaded that he led us there with the intention of causing us all our deaths.

The second ambassador scolded these persons severely, saying that the poor man did all he could, and the great services he had rendered us in such difficult circumstances, without any obligation on his part, should not be paid for with such a horrible crime. As with difficulties which at first sight astonish naturally timid persons become less evident when seen close up, so these places we considered from afar as so dangerous did not appear so when we travelled further, and when we climbed them it seemed that the slope was more gentle. In spite of all our troubles, exhaustion, hunger, and thirst, we managed to get through.

Throughout that time we only lived off a few mussels dried in the sun, which we conserved as much as we could; and we were happy when we came across some particular small green trees, the leaves of which had a special sharp taste which seemed to us very tasty; they formed a great stew, mixed with our dried mussels. A kind of green frog known as *raines* also seemed to us most exquisite and very tasty. We had already eaten some before when travelling along a track with lots of greenery on which they fed, and we found them fairly frequently, on which occasions we did not hesitate to make use of them, as with grasshoppers which are nowhere near so palatable. I have no difficulty in proclaiming that the insect which seemed to us the most tasty was a kind of large, completely black fly or cockchafer, which is only found in and lives upon refuse. We found many in the dung of elephants alongside the path on which the Hottentot took us, through valleys and mountains. The only preparation which we took before eating them was to grill them over a fire, and we found them delicious. This knowledge might be useful for those who find themselves in the dire straits in which we had remained so long.

SALVATION

Finally, on the thirty-first day of our overland journey after our unfortunate shipwreck, and the sixth after we had happily come across the Hottentots I have spoken about, about ten in the morning when coming down a hill, we saw four persons on top of a very high mountain before us, and which we had to cross. The first time we saw them, we took them to be Hottentots, because at the distance we were from them we could not distinguish them clearly, and we did not think there could be any other persons around. As they approached us, and we them, we were agreeably undeceived and easily saw that there were two Dutchmen, and the two others were the Hottentots whom we had left four days earlier, to go ahead and give warning of our presence to the Dutch. At this sight we suddenly felt an extraordinary joy. It seemed to us as though we had found our liberators, and we were persuaded that after having endured so many afflictions our lives were assured.

This joyous feeling increased when they came up to us. The first thing they asked us was if we were Siamese, and where were the ambassadors of the king our master, and the letter they were bearing.[14] When they were shown them, the two Dutchmen paid them many compliments, after which, indicating that we should be seated, they had the two Kaffirs with them approach with some victuals for us. When we saw that they brought fresh bread, cooked meat, and wine,[15] we were unable to restrain our gratitude. Some threw themselves at their feet and kissed their knees, others called them their fathers and liberators; in short there was not one of us who did not show them signs of most particular friendship.

In my case, I was so overwhelmed that I wanted to show them immediately how much I was touched by the kindness they

14. As will be seen below, the Portuguese had arrived at the Cape a week before the Siamese, and announced their probable arrival.

15. Fresh bread and wine are unlikely to be the first thoughts of a Siamese *khunnang* after thirty-one days without food. See note 13.

showed. The first ambassador, when he ordered us to leave him on the wayside and go and find some carriage to bring him to the Cape, handed over several precious stones which the king our master had given him in order to make various gifts. He gave me five large diamonds, mounted in as many gold rings. When I saw that these Dutchmen were so generous in their refreshments, I presented each of them with one of these rings to thank them for the life they restored to me.

I do not know if what I am going to say will be believed, though I was not only witness to it, but experienced it myself. But the truth is in the nature of those things which have little verisimilitude, and can only be believed relunctantly and with caution. But since I am relating all the events which occurred during our sad journey, I shall not hesitate to add this, requiring no one to heed or believe my word. When the Dutchmen had given us something to eat, and we had drunk a little of the wine they brought, we felt so weak, and found it was impossible to bring ourselves to proceed further; not one of us could rise except with greatest difficulty and incredible pain. In a word, although the two Dutchmen told us that there was only one hour's walk to bring us to their dwellings where we could rest at leisure, none of our group had sufficient strength nor sufficient courage to move to get there. Later on, thinking about this surprising situation, so contrary to what could normally be expected of this encounter, I could find no other reason than that I give here, which came into my mind of its own accord, leaving the decision [about its interpretation] to those who have greater knowledge or understanding than I.

When we thought we were in danger of dying, we only tried to save ourselves by forcing ourselves to walk; this terrible fear made such an impression on our minds that it gave us strength, in spite of our extreme weakness, to make considerable efforts. What does one not do to save oneself from an immediate danger, when one is threatened with a cruel and squalid death? Throughout our journey we only thought of freeing ourselves from the extreme misery which weighed daily ever more heavily on us.

The cerastes or horned viper

Chameleon of the Cape

The terrible fate of our companions whom we had been obliged to abandon in the forests, or whom we had lost; the horrible death of those we passed prostrate along the wayside, inspired such fear in us and gave us renewed strength. Moreover, the hope we had, especially after meeting these three Hottentots, that we would soon be freed from our afflictions caused us to think each day that the next day our salvation would be assured, and we persuaded ourselves each morning on setting out that by the evening we would have arrived at the Cape of Good Hope. Such diverse thoughts constantly preoccupied our minds, and filled our imagination with fancies that were sometimes frightening, sometimes agreeable. We made continual efforts and overcame all kinds of difficulties without being detained by the perils and obstacles which confronted us, nor by the terrible pains which afflicted us. On the contrary, as soon as we were no longer sustained by such great visions, and were delivered from the fear of dying, and our hopes realized, it is not surprising that our hearts gave over to joy and the gentleness of an easy and tranquil life which had been the case in the past; one should not be surprised, say I, if our hearts weakened by such sentiments did not have the courage to continue and to surmount the same obstacles which we had overcome shortly before only under pressure from the powerful motives which I have described.[16]

Whatever the case, the two Dutchmen, seeing that they could not get us to take one step more in spite of whatever they said, sent off the Hottentots to fetch carriages to transport us. In less than two hours they had returned, and we saw two carts arrive, as well as a few horses. The horses were of no use that day; no one could mount them, and we all got onto the carts which took us to a Dutch dwelling at about a league from the foot of the mountain. This was truly a safe haven and a house of repose. We spent the night there sleeping on the straw with incredible pleasure and indulgence. What joy we had on waking to find

16. This philosophical digression seems more likely to stem from the Jesuit Tachard than from Ok-khun Chamnan.

ourselves under shelter, far from the terrible dangers we had endured for thirty-one days.

Our first concern on arriving in the evening at that house was to request the Dutchman who was the owner to send off a cart with necessary victuals to seek out the seven Siamese we had left behind, as I have already related. After the departure of this cart, we climbed into two others, which took us to a Dutch dwelling some four or five leagues away from the first. The [Dutch East Indies] Company raises in those parts an infinity of cattle and sheep, and even a large number of horses.

ARRIVAL AT THE CAPE

Some time after we had arrived, we were informed that the governor was sending several soldiers to act as an escort for us, and two horses for the two ambassadors; but they were so sick, as much as the rest of us, that they did not dare mount them. So after using the same carts as before, we arrived in this state at the fortress which the Dutch have in the roads of the Cape of Good Hope. The governor had been warned of our arrival and sent his secretary to receive the ambassadors before we entered the fortress, and to offer them his compliments. This secretary conducted us into the fort, passing some twenty soldiers lined up near the guardhouse, and took us into the governor's residence. The governor himself was waiting at the foot of the staircase built externally to the house, and received with considerable respect and warmth the ambassadors and the mandarins in their suite. He had us enter a room where, after we were seated, tea and wine were served, and eleven cannon shots were fired to honour the king our master in the person of his ambassadors.

We entreated him urgently to despatch people with some victuals for the first ambassador whom we had left quite close to the shore where we were shipwrecked, for we hoped he would still be alive. He said that in the rainy season, which now prevailed, it was impossible to send anyone, but that when the weather changed for the better, he would not fail to take all possible measures to seek out this ambassador, and provide for him all the necessary means for his return. He added that we were lucky to have followed the shoreline, for if we had ventured somewhat into the forests, we would certainly have fallen into the hands of certain Kaffirs who spare no one, and who would have massacred us without pity in order to eat us, as they were very fond of human flesh. At the end of the conversation he indicated that he was most distressed by the accident which had befallen us, and on learning of all the privations we had suffered, but he could assure us that we had found in him a person to whom it would be a real pleasure to cause us to forget all our previous woes by the good treatment we would receive; he considered himself happy to find an occasion in which he could demonstrate the respect and gratitude which the Dutch Company had always had for the great benefits which it had received from the king our master.

As soon as we had got near the Cape, and seen the ships in the roads, we experienced the consoling hope that we should see once again our family and friends, and our dear country; and these words of the governor agreeably confirmed this gentle thought. This assurance removed from our minds almost all the memories of our past troubles. So we thanked him with all the gratitude and civility possible. He kept his word very faithfully: he ordered his secretary to bring us to the residence he had prepared for us in the settlement, where he had us provided very liberally, as it turned out, with all the victuals we needed. It is true that he kept a very exact account of the expenses we incurred, which he sent to the ministers of the king our master, who reimbused him according to his accounts for all his expenditures as was due; these charges included the rent for our residence, and the pay of the officers and soldiers who had gone ahead of us, and who subsequently mounted guard at the door of our house throughout the time we stayed there.[17]

17. The Dutch VOC was a trading company where the bottom line of profit reigned supreme.

Small lizard of the Cape

Large lizard of the Cape

THE FATE OF THE PORTUGUESE

The Portuguese had arrived at the Cape eight days before us, after suffering even more discomfort than we did. A Portuguese Father of the order of Saint Augustin who accompanied, on the king's orders, the Portuguese ambassadors,[18] gave us an account which brought tears into our eyes. He said that one had to be as pitiless as the tigers not to have one's heart broken by the cries and groans of the poor people who fell by the wayside, overcome by the terrible suffering which the swelling of their bodies and legs caused, and the hunger and thirst which drove them to distraction. They cried out for the assistance of their friends, and their dear ones; they implored them to give them a little water. Everyone by then was insensible of their groanings, and heedless of what one did in order not to appear cruel and barbarous when someone fell down, which occurred several times a day; they were encouraged to commend their souls to God, without saying any more, and averted their gaze from them and blocked their ears for fear of being frightened by the dreadful cries which resounded on all sides because of the large number of dying persons who collapsed at almost every hour of the day; for on this journey, as soon as they left us, to proceed more quickly, they lost fifty or sixty persons of all ages and condition, without counting those who had died beforehand, among whom was a Jesuit Father who was already greatly broken down by age.

But the saddest occurrence which could be imagined, the like of which one has perhaps never seen, was what happened to the captain of our ship. He was a person of quality and considerable wealth, had long been a ship's captain, and had given valliant service to the king his master on numerous occasions, in which

18. This refers to the embassy sent to Siam by Pedro II mentioned at the beginning of Chamnan's account. The Portuguese are unlikely to have sent more than one ambassador *per se*, who would have had the usual retinue. It is curious that this is the only reference to the embassy which apparently returned from Siam with the Siamese embassy, at least as far as Goa.

he gave all the proofs of his valour and probity. I do not recall his surname; but I have often heard that there was hardly a more illustrious family in the whole of Portugal. This gentleman had taken to the Indies his only son, aged about ten or twelve years, either because he wanted him to learn his profession at an early age, and accustom him from his youth to the perils of the sea, or he was not prepared to hand over to another the education of his child, whom he cherished more than himself. Indeed this boy had all the qualities that were needed to make one love him, for he was a handsome youth, very polite, knowledgeable for his years, and as respectful, gentle, and tender for his father as it was possible to be. His father, when he went ashore from the shipwreck, had taken him himself to be sure of his safety. During their journey he had him carried by slaves, but in the end all these negroes had died on the way, or were so weak that they could not drag forward even themselves. Three days after the Portuguese had left us, this poor child had become so weak and swollen, that one afternoon, resting on a rock, still more exhausted than all the others, he was unable to get up again; he was stretched out with his legs so stiff he could neither raise nor bend them. This sight was like a dagger in the heart of his father; he tried several times to raise him, he was held up a while to try to make his blood flow, but his legs could no longer support him. He was dragged along, and those whom the father had asked to share this task with him, seeing that they could not continue either, frankly said to the captain that they could not carry him further without perishing with him. This poor man was reduced to despair, and wished to carry his son himself, and put him on his shoulders, but he did not have the strength to move one step ahead, and fell with his son, who seemed more affected by the pains of his father than his own. He implored him many times to let him die, and said that if he were carried further, he could not survive the night, and that the affliction of his father, and the tears he shed were infinitely more painful than all the suffering he endured. These words, far from deciding the captain to withdraw, made him still more affectionate, and he took the decision to die with his son. This boy, surprised at his father's resolution, and seeing he could not persuade him to change his mind, spoke to the other Portuguese, urgently requesting them in words which broke their hearts, to take his father away, since his presence increased his anguish and the pains he felt, and the sight of whom would hasten his death.

A Father of the order of St Augustin, and another of the order of St Francis, went up to the captain and said he could not, in all conscience, carry out his resolution; he was obliged to save his own life, and if he died in this manner he would be damned forever. Then all the Portuguese took him off by force, and took him a few paces out of sight of his son, who had been placed a little to one side. This separation was so brutal and so distressing to the ship's captain that he never got over it; his suffering was so continual and intense that he died of grief one or two days after arriving at the Cape.

RETURN TO SIAM

We stayed nearly four months at the Cape of Good Hope, waiting for a Dutch ship to take us to Batavia. The misery we had endured had so afflicted us that we took more than two months to regain our strength. I think that without the help of the surgeon, who took good care of us, not one of us would have recovered. We had to fast at first, although it was extremely difficult not to fill our stomachs with food which would have been too much for us; we had to fast, I say, in spite of ourselves, for I can aver that we found it more difficult not to satisfy our hunger, seeing we were able to do so, than when we had to endure extreme hunger when there was nothing to eat.

Before leaving the Cape, we learnt that the second pilot of the Portuguese ship had escaped on an English vessel; the first pilot wanted to do the same, but the ship's master, with the crew which remained, confined him so closely that he could not make his escape; they wanted to bring him to Portugal, and punish him for his negligence. Most of the Portuguese went aboard Dutch ships which took them to Amsterdam, from where they were due to travel on to Portugal; others took, like us, a ship of the Dutch Company which had come late in the season to the Cape, and which transported us all to Batavia, where each of us made shift for himself. We arrived there in November, after leaving the Cape at the beginning of September.[19] We set sail for Siam in June [1687], where we arrived the following September. The king our master received us with marks of benevolence and extraordinary kindness. He gave us clothes and money, and gave us to understand that he would not forget us when the occasion presented itself to improve our fortune.

I had only been back six months in Siam when the envoys extraordinary from the King of France arrived at the bar [of Siam].[20] Oia Wichayen (that is, Mr Constance),[21] the chief minister of the king my master, ordered me to go and greet them on his behalf, and thank them for the honour they showed him in their letter, and in the gentleman they had sent ahead.[22] What procured me this advantage was that during my travels I had learnt enough Portuguese to speak the language and make myself

19. Again Chamnan/Tachard's figures do not add up. If the shipwreck occcured on 27 April 1686 and the group spent thirty-one days travelling overland from Cape Agulhas to the Dutch settlement at the Cape of Good Hope, followed by nearly four months at the settlement, that means they left for Batavia at the end of September rather than the beginning. Seven months waiting for a ship to travel from Batavia to Siam was not unusual.

20. The dates once more are suspect. La Loubère and Céberet, the envoys extraordinary, arrived at the bar of Siam on 26 September 1687, and Chamnan says he returned to Siam in September 1687, so he could hardly have been back six months before the envoys arrived.

21. Oia (Oya, Ok-ia, or Ok-ya) Wichayen was the Siamese title given by King Narai to Phaulkon. He did not have the title of chief minister or even *phra klang*, minister of foreign affairs and trade, but he filled the functions of minister from about 1683 to his death in 1688.

22. Céberet records in October 1687 the arrival of "two *ok-khun* from the palace", one of whom was Chamnan Chaichong. See introduction, pp. 4–5. The person sent ahead was the Sieur de Mazuyer, also spelt Mazuier and Mazurier.

understood; and this fact caused Father Tachard to ask His Majesty for my services. Although I was not completely recovered from the ordeals I had suffered, nevertheless the fine things that the mandarins proclaimed who came from France[23] gave rise a great desire in me to learn the truth for myself. But what caused me most to undertake such a long journey was the desire to see the greatest and most powerful monarch in the world, whose extraordinary virtues and great reputation are well known and admired even in the most distant lands.[24]

23. The mandarins who returned from France included Kosa Pan (Ok-phra Wisut Sunthorn), Ok-luang Kanlaya Ratchamaitri, and Ok-khun Sisawan Wacha, the first, second, and third ambassadors to France.

24. This puff for Louis XIV is undoubtedly more Tachard's than Chamnan's. Tachard dedicated his *Second Voyage* to Louis XIV, perhaps hoping for admission to the Académie Française on the strength of this and his first *Voyage de Siam*. However, the person he disliked most, La Loubère, was so elected in 1693 after the publication of his masterpiece *Du Royaume de Siam* in 1691, for which he collected his material on his return journey to France in 1688.

Namaqua, newly discovered people

POSTSCRIPT

We appear to have only Tachard's word that Ok-khun Chamnan's story is correct. Tachard is less economical of the truth, as the phrase goes, than inventive of it. Céberet, a director-general of the French East Indies Company, in a notable story, gleefully cited by the Missionary Fr Vachet, whom Tachard had done his best to sideline in Siamese affairs, and who in addition spoke fluent Siamese, accused Tachard of lying in his *Second voyage* . . . After running through all the persons who had nothing good to say about Tachard (the list is long), Vachet accused the Jesuit of being "a swindler and an imposter who imposed on the Court and the public by the accounts he has had printed." The account of the story concerning Céberet runs thus:

Fr Tachard, going one day to pay a visit to the Director who was working in his office, and waiting for him to come out, had the curiosity to open a book which he found on the table in the waiting room. Delighted to find it was his most recent publication, he wanted to leaf through some parts. But on opening the book, he was strangely surprised to see in the margin of the first page which came before his eyes the word "Lie" at five different places, and what increased his astonishment was to notice that all pages, without exception, bore this remark, some more than others. He still had the book in his hand when

Mr Céberet appeared and said to him, on greeting him: "What good book are you reading there, Father?"

"In truth," Fr Tachard replied, "it is the account which I gave the public of the journey to Siam which I undertook in your wake, but I cannot guess the meaning of this great number of 'Lies' which are in the margins, written by you, for I know your writing."

"Father," replied Mr Céberet, "they represent as many falsehoods as you have passed off for truths, and which only exist in a brain as disordered as yours. I regret to have to tell you this, but also I am obliged to complain, since you have called me to witness so many untruths as it pleased you to invent."

Any person other than Fr Tachard would have been covered in confusion. But his particular genius, which renders him shameless, allowed the reproach to slide off his back, as if it were something which did not concern him . . . (unpublished section of Vachet's Mémoires, in the archives of the Foreign Missions in Paris, MEP vol. 112/2, pp. 239–240)

We also know that Tachard's account of the death of Fr d'Espagnac, taken captive at Tavoy on fleeing from Mergui in 1688 and condemned to perpetual slavery in Pegu, sometime before March 1692, was imaginative. All that was known for certain was that he had died. Tachard wrote:

After a thousand cruel torments which he suffered in the Kingdom of Pegu, he was sent to Ava, capital of a kingdom of the same name much further inland. Although he was a slave, he had begun to convert some people to Christianity, when the idolaters accused him before the magistrates of conspiring against the state and of associating with supporters. On this accusation he was shamefully driven out of the town and all nearby refuges. Thus he was obliged to withdraw into the forest, exposed to hunger, thirst, snakes, and tigers. It was never known for sure in what way he ended his life after so much suffering (Tachard, Relation de voyage aux Indes 1690–1699, unpublished ms in the Bibliothèque Nationale, Fr. 19030, 1er cahier, p. 24)

Only the last sentence above is true; the rest embroidery. Even to Pope Innocent XI, Tachard could not tell the truth. At his audience on 23 December 1688, with Ok-khun Chamnan and his companions present, he had this to say about King Narai:

> This powerful monarch, has already begun to take instruction [in the Christian religion], he constructs altars and churches in the name of the true God, he asks for zealous and learned missionaries, and builds magnificent houses and colleges for them . . . Never, Holy Father, have the Gospels of Jesus Christ had such great opportunities to be established so solidly. (Tachard 1689: 405)

The first and last phrases are quite untrue, for the Siamese king was not receiving instruction from anyone, nor was the church making any progress in conversions among the mandarinate or the people. The rest are half-truths. Narai did not establish large numbers of Christian foundations, only a church in Ayutthaya and Lopburi, and a Jesuit establishment in each (in addition to the older house of the Missions Etrangères and its college in Ayutthaya), and did not seek more missionaries as such, only men of science.

Could the whole story of Chamnan's shipwreck be a fabrication, used to fill pages in Tachard's book which was already puffed out with texts from numerous other cited sources?

While one should take everything Tachard writes with more than one pinch of salt, it seems rather unlikely he would have invented the whole story of a Siamese embassy to Portugal, its shipwreck, and Chamnan's adventures travelling overland from Cape Agulhas to the Cape of Good Hope. There would be simpler ways of explaining Chamnan's knowledge of Portuguese, said to be acquired in his eleven-month stay in Goa. Furthermore, as Tachard himself says (1689: 309), Chamnan was in Paris at the time his book was published, and it would have been easy for the incredulous to check on his story.

But one has to admit that the dates provided by Tachard in Chamnan's account do not accord with the lengths of time Chamnan says he passed in various places. As indicated in the notes, several of Chamnan's supposed philosophical reflections, be it on the value of life, on God, the difficulty of moving once a safe haven was in sight, to his lack of shoes and stockings and the absence or availability of bread and wine, are all European reactions rather than those of a Siamese *khunnang*, no matter how long he had stayed in Goa beforehand.

Access to Goan and Portuguese sources might confirm the stay of the Siamese embassy for most of 1685 en route to Lisbon. Checking the Dutch records of VOC activities at the Cape would confirm the arrival of the remnants of the Siamese embassy to Lisbon and the sending of a bill to Siam for the upkeep of the rump embassy while there. Similarly, Dutch records of movements in Batavia might reveal the passage of a Siamese party for six months in 1687.

Fortunately there are two Dutch records which confirm Tachard's story, and I am deeply grateful to Dr. Dhiravat Na Pombejra of Chulalongkorn University, Bangkok, for locating these. The first is in the Algemeen Rijksarchief, VOC 1440: Letter of Joannes Keijts and Council in Ayutthaya to Governor-General Camphuijs and Council [Batavia], 1 November 1687, mentioning the imprisonment and torture of the second Siamese ambassador to Portugal, "Loang Samrett Maitrij" (Ok-luang Samret Maitri?) upon the envoy's return to Siam. This ambassador was accused of many things, the most important among which were that he had wanted—upon finally reaching Goa—to "throw overboard" the King of Siam's "commission" because he did not want to face the rigours of a trip all the way to Europe, and also that he had abandoned the first ambassador,

"Opra Visuta Sinea" (?), in "the forests of the Cape" to be the prey of wild animals [folio 2230]. This is the selfsame second ambassador who made such a point of protecting and guarding the king's letter in the Tachard-Chamnan version of the tale.

The second record, also VOC 1440: Letter of Okya Phrasadet Surenthrathibodi (acting *phra klang*) to Governor-General Camphuijs and Council [Batavia], 18 January 1688, thanks the VOC for helping the shipwrecked Portugal-bound envoys of the King of Siam return to Siam in safety [folio 2509].

These two documents alone prove that Ok-khun Chamnan Chaichong's story is based on fact, and only some of its details appear to have been distorted by Tachard.

Views of Table and Lion Mountains

PART TWO

THREE CONTEMPORARY
DESCRIPTIONS
OF THE CAPE OF GOOD HOPE

The Portuguese navigator, Vasco da Gama (c.1469–1524), discovered the route to India round the Cape of Good Hope in 1497–8; Goa was seized by Affonso de Albuquerque in 1510, as was Malacca the following year. But it was the Dutch East India Company, the VOC, which in 1652 first settled at the Cape. When the first French embassy to Siam called there in 1685, the settlement was only just over thirty years old, and in consequence was extremely small. As can be seen from the contemporary French accounts which follow, the Dutch made good use of this settlement, a vital refuelling and refreshment stop on the way to Batavia in Java, which they had seized in 1619.

The Abbé de Choisy (1644–1724) was co-adjutant ambassador to the Chevalier de Chaumont on the first French embassy to Siam. He recorded the embassy's stay at the Cape on the way to Ayutthaya, from 1 to 7 June 1685, and on its return, from 12 to 26 March 1686 (two months before Ok-khun Chamnan and his party arrived), in his daily journal to his friend the Abbé de Dagneau. This was first published as *Journal du Voyage de Siam* in 1687, but an English translation did not appear until 1993.

His stay coincided with that of Guy Tachard (1648–1712), who was on board the same ship, the *Oiseau*, as one of six Jesuits travelling as mathematicians from Louis XIV and bound for China. He became embroiled in Siamese affairs, however, in concert with Constantine Phaukon, the Levantine adventurer who was an important if not the chief minister in Siam from

1683 until his murder in 1688. Tachard left a very full account of the settlement at the Cape, puffed out with pages of boring information concerning the readings of the stars and emersions of Jupiter's satellites, the purpose of which was to show that the Jesuits were adept at astonomical calculations and that the maps indicating the location of the Cape were slightly inaccurate. His account, published as *Voyage de Siam . . .* 1686 is given here, without the astronomical calculations.

Tachard returned to Siam with the following French mission in 1687 led by the envoys extraordinary Simon de La Loubère and Claude Céberet; by then he had managed to make himself ambassador in all but name. But he spares us a further description of the Cape, merely indicating in his *Second Voyage...* of 1688 that he met the same governor as two years previously. He adds that there was a fire in the settlement on the outward journey which French soldiers ashore helped extinguish, and that Frs de Bèze and Le Blanc had tried to calculate the height of Table Mountain. On the return journey Tachard noted there were fifteen VOC ships in the harbour, as well as three French vessels. A number of French Protestants expelled by the revocation of the Edict of Nantes in 1685 were en route to settle in the Indies; he claimed they all regretted their decision to leave France.

La Loubère (1643–1729), in his *Du Royaume de Siam*, published in 1691, included in the second part of his book a section on the Dutch settlement at the Cape. La Loubère and Tachard (who intensely disliked him, an antipathy reciprocated) were in the Cape from 11 to 25 June 1687 and again, on the return journey, from 21 April to 1 May 1688. La Loubère's account of the Cape and its inhabitants is the most succinct and the least patronizing of the indigenous peoples there.

ABBÉ FRANÇOIS-TIMOLÉON
DE CHOISY

Journal of a Voyage to Siam 1685–1686, translated and introduced by Michael Smithies, Kuala Lumpur, Oxford University Press, 1993, pp. 79–83, 260–265. Reprinted with permission.

1 JUNE [1685]
[Friday]

In the roads of the Cape there are four ships taking a Commissioner-General to the Indies from the Dutch East India Company who will inspect its ports and put everything in order. He is called Baron van Reede,[1] and has absolute authority, even to change governors. This morning he sent a gentleman to pay his compliments to the Ambassador.[2] The ship carrying him flies an Admiral's flag. Thus the Dutch do in the seas of the Indies, and as soon as they have crossed the Line, they fly the flag even if it is only a small merchant vessel. The Ambassador sent the Chevalier de Forbin[3] to present his compliments to the

1. Henrik-Adriaan van Reede tot Drakestein (1636–1691), lord of Mijdrecht, had in 1685 just been named commissioner-general by the seventeen directors of the Verenigde Oostindische Compagnie (VOC). He was highly intelligent and an enthusiastic botanist, who compiled a *Hortus Malabaricus*.
2. The ambassador was the Chevalier de Chaumont (c.1640–1710).
3. Chevalier Claude de Forbin (1656–1733) entered the navy when very

Commissioner-General and to the Governor.[4] We greeted the fort with a seven gun salute and were replied in kind. All the vessels in the roads, their Admiral included, greeted us with seven, five, or three gun salutes. We in turn replied; each gave thanks with a single shot. Our invalids, our Jesuits, and our Missionaries went on land. I shall go tomorrow in good company, for they say there are on the mountainside some bad-tempered lions and extremely impertinent wild elephants.

The Commissioner-General has just sent to the Ambassador a present of fruit, vegetables, and fish. We shall eat some salad; I do not care about the rest.

2 JUNE

This Commissioner-General is a gentleman; he has just sent a dozen fat sheep. I went on land this morning. The fortress is very attractive. The dwellings consist of houses mostly covered in thatch, but so clean and so white that you know they are Dutch. There is a garden which the Company has laid out; I would love it to be in a corner of Versailles. As far as the eye can see there are walks of orange and lemon trees, vegetable gardens, espaliers, and dwarf trees, the whole interspersed with fresh-water springs. All the fruit is laid out in the warehouse, and nothing leaves but for the Company's vessels.

All our youths went off hunting. They were provided with horses, dogs, and hunters to lead them to the right places. The lions and elephants have gone further away since the country became more populated, but the monkeys stayed on the mountain. They love melons; sometimes two hundred of them commandeer them from the gardens. First of all they place four or five guards on some rocks or in the trees; these send up a special cry when

---

young and became a ship's captain in 1689; he spent a year in Bangkok as governor 1685–86; he was later created count by Louis XIV.

4. Simon van der Stel (1639–1712) was born in Mauritius where his father was governor. He was commander at the Cape from 1679–1691, and held the title of governor from 1691–1699.

they see people. The bravest macaques come into the garden one behind the other, and pass the melons down the line. They return on three legs, each holding a melon, and when they are chased, they put the melon down very carefully, and defend themselves by throwing stones. This happens here several times every year. There was a big monkey in the fortress this morning who was hit by at least twenty stones without being felled. I think he would be rather good at tennis.

Our hunters have just come back loaded with deer and partridges. They were entertained at a house two leagues from here. They found many dwellings, a lot of game, but the countryside rough. They walked all day up to the neck in grasses and reeds; they will sleep soundly. For out part we went off to fish; it is a gentle pleasure, but none the worse for that. All the fish we caught were admirable, solid, fat, and tasting good; perhaps we are famished, but they seem better than your turbots.

3 JUNE

Water will be brought on board tomorrow, Tuesday the wood; on Wednesday everyone will be re-embarked. The men down with scurvy are already strong, and if it pleases God, on Thursday we set sail. We are mighty fine here, but must go to Siam.

I shall sleep on land in the Jesuit pavilion, in the middle of one of the finest gardens in the world. These good fathers had hardly appeared but the Commissioner-General offered to put them up, and to give them a place appropriate to stellar observation. They took him at his word. Their quarters are between two terraces, where there is plenty of room for the biggest telescopes; bread, wine, fruit, they lack nothing. They keep a good table. Are they foolish? They show the Dutch Jupiter's satellites, Saturn's belts, and the Milky Way. They have some small microscopes, in which can be seen such nice tiny images. I think that if they wanted to stay here, a house would be built for them. The intellect is a fine thing in all countries.

4 JUNE

This evening we took a good observation, and think we have corrected the longitude of the Cape of Good Hope. It is three degrees less to the east than had been thought. However, three degrees in longitude in these lands means forty-eight leagues, and that is most important when sailing. Here is the proof. The occulation of the moon occurred on 4 June at 10 hours 40 minutes in the evening, and in consequence seventy-four minutes later than in Paris. During the seventy-four minutes the moon only moved 18 degrees and a half; consequently the Cape is only 18 degrees and a half further east than Paris, whereas the maps usually place it 3 degrees further east. This single observation justifies all the instruments which the King has caused to have made. Do you not consider me a great astronomer? I was not totally useless in all this; whilst Father de Fontaney[5] was at his telescope and the others were in charge of the clocks, I called out from time to time, "One, two, three, four," to mark the seconds.

5 JUNE

I went this morning to return the visit of the Commissioner-General. The ambassador was restrained by his office; but I am of no consequence, and went to thank him for all his attentions to the French party. He received me admirably. He is a man in his sixties who is very similar to the late Mr de Navailles:[6] a fine countenance and much wit. He spoke Portuguese and I French; we had no need of an interpreter. He is very well advised of the interests of heads of state; it was very useful to me to have been your student. The conversation never flagged; it nearly always centred around the King, of whose great qualities he is aware as if he had spent all his life at Versailles. "Your King," he told me, "speaks as the Holy Writ: he pronounces and it is done. You tell

5. Fr Jean de Fontaney (1643–1710) was the superior of the six Jesuits travelling to China via Siam.
6. Philippe de Montault, Duke and Marshal of Navailles, died in 1684, aged 65.

me he spends four or five hours daily in Council; I think he spends all his time there, from the way he treats the nearby states." We took tea two or three times. Mr de Saint-Martin[7] came in. He is French, a Major-General commanding all the Company's troops in the Indies. He has just come from Holland and is returning to Batavia. These two men are very close to each other. More than thirty years ago, young, poor, unimportant, but brave, they embarked, musket on shoulder, on a ship going to the Indies. Since that time they have risen through the ranks to the greatest positions in the state. They had a friend whose luck had begun as far back as theirs and who died two years ago Governor of the Cape of Good Hope. They are going to erect a magnificent tomb to him, with an inscription which would explain the good fortune of the three friends.

Two wounded men and a dead tiger have just been brought in from a place two leagues from here. The two men were travelling with an armed gun each; the tiger leapt on one and the other immediately fired, but wounded his companion; the furious animal then turned on the person who had fired. The other, unencumbered though wounded, shot it between the eyes and killed it. I do not know if all this is lucid, but it is at least true. The Ambassador went to walk in the garden *incognito*: he met there the Dutch Generals. Much bowing and many compliments on both sides. It was by pure chance that they met,[8] and both parties were very pleased to make the other's acquaintance. I was their mutual confident.

I came on board this evening to sleep and we sail tomorrow.

6 JUNE
All the officers came back last night from the hunt with partridges as big and succulent as hens, small roe deer, and turtle-doves. Everything is good here, both meat and fish.

---

7. Isaac de l'Ostal de Saint-Martin (c.1629–1691), from Bearne, interested in history, languages, and botany, was in Dutch service in Batavia as early as 1662.
8. This is to be doubted.

The departing cannon shot has been fired; we are going to set sail. But it did not depend on us; no wind, we had to stay put. We were the better for it by small suckling pigs and wine from the Canary Islands, which the Commissioner-General sent us.

7 JUNE

At daybreak, we set sail with a good nor'westerly. We had to tack to leave the roads, but as the wind was not strong we did not have as much difficulty as on entering . . .

***

12 MARCH 1686
[Tuesday]

At daybreak we recognized Table Mountain. We were rather far out, because all night we went west. Now we must get closer to shore. We can see a ship going to the Cape; it would be rather amusing if she were the *Maligne*.[9] You remember that when we were going we found her at the entrance to the Straits of Sunda. Tomorrow, if it pleases God, we shall eat salad.

We entered the bay of the Cape quite successfully, and were going to anchor, when such a terrible wind blew up that we had to bring in all the sails, and leave only the foresail, and with a rear wind go towards Robben Island. There we found the *Maligne* anchored; she had done the same manoeuvre as us, and had been obliged to give up; now we are anchored next to her. The gloom and heavy sea prevent us from using the longboats. Tomorrow we shall relate our adventures to each other, and if God wills, and if the wind changes, we shall go to anchor in front of the fort. It is a good two leagues from here.

9. The *Maligne*, captained by Joyeaux, was the sister ship to the *Oiseau* carrying the French ambassadors.

13 MARCH

Mr Joyeaux came on board, and told us that he left us because in the first blast of wind his foresail was torn away, and he had to go with a following wind. He went through three storms like us, and took a more northerly route; he saw land below Cape Agulhas.[10] We have a Dutchman anchored next to us which has come from Batavia and is going to Europe. She had all the time the best possible weather, because she took the southern route. The Chevalier de Sibois[11] is going to Robben Island to look for some provisions; it is said there are plenty of cabbages there.

The wind is coming from the quarter. We hove to in order to go and anchor beneath the Cape fort. The Dutchman does the same. Sibois came back. The Governor of Robben Island showed him a thousand civilities, and told him our King has married the Infanta of Portugal; I do not believe it.

Now we are anchored, and the *Maligne* as well. We must go and stretch our legs a little in the fine garden I think I have already pompously described to you. When we came, it was a winter garden; and now it will be an autumn garden, where we should find fruit from all parts of the world. As for me, I have a penchant for early peaches, and prefer them to the durian, the mangosteen, and the pineapple.

Sibois has come from the Cape. The Governor offers everything at his disposition. We greeted the fort with a seven gun salute; it thanked us likewise. Then the Admiral of the Dutch fleet gave us a seven gun salute, which we returned, and finally the fort again gave us seven rounds.

14 MARCH

Life on board ship is very active. When you are sailing, it is all hauling up, trimming, anchoring, port, starboard, straight ahead, like this, slacken the tiller; there is always work. Hardly have you

---

10. Cape Agulhas is the southernmost point of Africa.

11. Chevalier de Sibois was a lieutenant on the *Oiseau* and succeeded Forbin, retained in Siam, as Chaumont's aide-de-camp for the return journey.

arrived in the right port, than you hear the hammer at work; the ship has been strained, it has to be repaired, strengthened, caulked, water taken on for three months, and the bottom of the hold has to be put in order. You do not have the time to be bored, and if one had nothing to do, no paper, no ink, no pen, just the questions 'What are they doing there?' would fill one's time.

A good dinner makes one forget three months of bad food. Soles in the European fashion, a big white fish with a trunk like an elephant, salads, grapes, melons, fresh eggs; we are going to try and refreshen ourselves. Then we shall keep ourselves warm from here to Brest; we shall have to go and freshen up again in Gournay.[12]

15 MARCH

The south-easterly is so terrible that we cannot go on shore. Three or four midshipmen were unable to return to sleep on board. The longboats do not dare attempt the trip. We have just seen a Dutchman turn turtle; the men were saved because they knew how to swim, people helped them, and the tide was going towards the shore. So here we are, as though on the high seas, without salad, without fish, without eggs; it is not pleasant at all.

The Governor of the Cape is rather offhand. The Ambassador has not yet heard from him; not the slightest little civility, still less provisions.

16 MARCH

The wind has abated somewhat, and very brave people can try to go on shore. I shall certainly go only when it is quite calm. To go and drown in a little bit of spittle after having gone to the

12. Gournay, to the east of Paris, was where Choisy's correspondent, the Abbé de Dagneau, had his living.

end of the earth! I am taking after good sailors and will be afraid of crossing the River Seine.

17 MARCH

Finally the Governor woke up, and has just sent the Ambassador his greetings along with two sheep, some melons, salads, and grapes; they come somewhat tardily and we shall not delay eating them. The weather is fine, and we are taking on as much water as we can.

18 MARCH

There was a frightful wind last night. We were straddled between two anchors; a third was let down for greater security, and a fourth was made ready. If these winds return so often, we look like not going ashore, but we do not care; there is nothing new to see. The garden is not as fine as it was last year; the summer heat will have somewhat dried it up, and we have all our provisions. If God grants us grace to reach France, we shall eat melons and grapes twice this year.

19 MARCH

Fine weather. The First Siamese Ambassador[13] went ashore; he was greeted with a nine gun salute when he got into the dinghy. He found the garden attractive, and swam in a pool, even though he was told the water from this spring would not be good for him; he returned with a heavy cold.

20 MARCH

I too went ashore, and have worn myself out with walking. The Hottentots amused us with a race, and by cleverly hitting each other with a staff, in return for a few Dutch ha'pennies.

The Governor of the Cape himself last year went exploring inland. He has forbidden under pain of death those who went

13. The first Siamese ambassador was Ok-phra Wisut Sunthorn, Kosa Pan.

with him to say what they had seen; we do not despair, nevertheless, of learning something.

21 MARCH

After carefully investigating the news of the marriage of the King with the Infanta of Portugal, we came up with nothing concrete, and I do not believe it at all.

22 MARCH

We shall complete taking on water today. Five hundred chickens are on board, fifty sheep, some very good dried fish; all our exposed parts are caulked. Who will stop you from sailing the day after Our Lady's feast?[14] And who told you we shall not see in France St. John's fire?[15]

The youngest of the Siamese ambassadors went ashore; he was treated to a seven gun salute.[16]

23 MARCH

It appears to be dully calm, but we hope that the wind will not fail us when we want it. I am worn out today after so much walking.

24 MARCH

A small Portuguese ship coming from Mozambique and going to Brazil put out its sails four times this afternoon, and each time had to anchor again for lack of wind. It is full of negroes and has a poor crew. The eight Dutchmen in the roads are waiting for four more from Batavia, to go together to Europe. They are tarred, and look quite new. We do not look so fine, but we have good swords. They will only leave in a fortnight. These gentle-

14. The festival of the Annunciation falls on 25 March.
15. Midsummer's Day, 24 June.
16. The youngest of the three Siamese ambassadors, the *trithut*, was Okkhun Siwisan Wacha.

men are never in a hurry; their captains are having fun on shore, and the sailors are taking on water at their convenience. They almost never row, but use their sails as much as possible.

25 MARCH

All our youth have gone ashore to hunt. One day running about a lot on land will compensate them for three months of rolling.

26 MARCH

I told you so. Hardly had our affairs been settled, and all our people on board, than a south-easterly sprang up, and with this we soon lost sight of the Cape. We have always left with a following wind and cover forty leagues a day.

27 MARCH

Our ship is rolling more than ever; there was no way of sleeping last night. We had become used to a quiet life; we must still suffer until we are two hundred leagues away from the Cape; after that it will be calmer than we would like. I shall tell you tomorrow all that I have picked up about the discoveries the Dutch have made around the Cape. But for today, enough, please.

28 MARCH

Last year the Governor of the Cape himself went exploring. He took with him sixty Dutchmen, two hundred slaves, some Hottentots, five horses, thirty-eight bullock carts, and 160 beasts of burden. He went, he said, two hundred leagues to the north, through a most miserable land, and found nothing remarkable, only a few people quite well-built, white, very friendly, who were always dancing. One day when he was encamped on a small eminence, the Hottentots who were with him came to tell him he was going to die, and they saw coming towards him the two greatest sorcerers in the land. In truth, two strangely dressed men, followed by a hundred others, came up very seriously; but he forestalled them and made them understand that he was a greater sorcerer than they. To prove this, he had brought before them a glass of brandy, which he set alight and swallowed burning. The poor sorcerers threw themselves down on their knees, recognized his power as superior, and withdrew. He also said that he thought he would have been killed by a rhinoceros, which are terrible there, and with their horn they dig up the earth when coming straight at you. They are only afraid of the sound of drums.

The Governor only said that, but he is not paid to tell us the secrets of the [Dutch India] Company. This is what one of those who accompanied him, a man of common sense, told us. They found the most beautiful country on earth, and this can be believed, because they took their wagons with them. The people are very gentle. There are gold and silver mines, and he gave us some samples. From time to time they found small hills entirely made of alabaster, and some entirely of crystal. These mines were more than 150 leagues from the Cape, three or four leagues from the sea. Finally, what makes us think that there is something there is that the Governor is sending a big boat to explore the coasts, and try to go up the rivers.

FATHER GUY TACHARD

Voyage de Siam des Pères Jésuites . . . , Paris, 1686, Amsterdam 1687, pp. 51–95, 169–171. Tachard relates the discoveries made by the governor between his first and second calls at the Cape in his first account of the Dutch outpost. The lengthy details of his astronomical observations have been omitted.

The Cape of Good Hope appears on approaching it from Europe as a long series of mountains stretching north to south, ending in a headland going into the sea. The first two peaks to be seen, ten leagues away from the headland, are the Table and Lion mountains. We saw Table Mountain first; it is so called because its top is very flat and looks rather like a table. Lion Mountain roughly resembles a lion lying on its side. Although it advances further into the sea than the other, we only saw it afterwards. From far off they seem to form one mountain, and they are not very far from each other. At the foot of these mountains a broad oval bay goes inland to the east, some two leagues wide at its entrance, and about nine leagues around. All the coast is safe to the south going towards the mountains, but it is wide open to attack on all other sides . . .

Near the middle of this bay, about a league inside it, the Dutch have built a pentagonal fort beneath Table Mountain, protecting it from the south, and behind Lion Mountain, which protects it from the west. One passes to the left on entering the bay a fairly low island callen Robben Island, in the middle of which the

The Jesuit Father Guy Tachard (1648 or 1651–1712), special envoy of Phra Narai in 1688 to Louis XIV and Pope Innocent XI, drawn by Carlo Maratta (1625–1713), in the Vatican Library (BAV, Vat. Lat. 14166).

Dutch have raised their flag. They banish from this land, and even from the Indies, the people they want to punish, having them make lime from the shells which the sea casts up there . . .

We anchored the next day [on Friday 1 June 1685] a hundred and fifty paces from the fort. There were in the roads of the Cape four large ships, which had arrived there a month before from Holland, though they had been at sea more than two months before us. The most important carried an admiral's pennant below its flag, as a mark of the supreme power that the Dutch East India Company gives itself in the Indies. She was commanded by Baron van Reede,[1] who was sent by the East India Company with the title of commissioner-general to visit all the strongholds which they control in the Indies. He had full power to order all things, to change the officers of factories, and even the governors of their strongholds if he thought fit. The second was commanded by Baron de Saint-Martin,[2] a Frenchman by birth, and major-general of Batavia, in that position commanding all the troops the United Provinces have in the Indies. Sieur Bocheros, an old sea captain and counsellor to Mr van Reede during the time of his commission, commanded the third, and the fourth waited on Mr de Saint-Martin, who was due to leave any time for Batavia.

All these gentlemen and Mr van der Stel,[3] governor, or to speak like the Dutch, commander of the Cape, are true gentlemen, and it was a fortuitous encounter for us, that we had to deal with them during our stay there.

We had hardly anchored before two boats came up to us to know who we were, and next morning about seven o'clock the commissioner-general sent his compliments to our ambassador,[4] who on his part ordered the Chevalier de Forbin,[5] the ship's

---

1. Henrik-Adriaan van Reede tot Drakestein (1636–1691). See note 1, p. 69.
2. Isaac de l'Ostal de Saint-Martin (c.1629–1691). See note 7, p. 72.
3. Simon van der Stel (1639–1712). See note 4, p. 69.
4. The ambassador was the Chevalier de Chaumont (c.1640–1710).
5. Chevalier Claude de Forbin (1656–1733). See note 3, p. 69.

lieutenant commander, and three other officers to go on shore and salute him, and also to request that we might take in fresh water and necessary provisions. He very civilly gave his consent, and on learning that there were several gentlemen in the ambassador's retinue, he invited them to come and hunt on shore. He enquired if there were any Jesuits on board our ships, for it is probable that those who had come the day before had noticed us, and talked of us on their return. Mr de Forbin replied that there were six of us going to China, and that there were some ecclesiastics on board bound for Siam.

Then they discussed the gun salutes, and it was agreed that the fort should return shot for shot after our ship saluted it. This matter was badly explained or badly understood by these gentlemen, for about ten o'clock, after our ambassador had ordered seven guns to be fired, the admiral only answered with five shots, and the fort fired none at all. Immediately the ambassador sent someone on shore again, and it was agreed that the admiral's salute would count for nothing, and so the fort fired seven shots, the admiral seven shots, and the other ships five, to salute the king's ship, which returned their salutation, for which the fort and ships gave their thanks. After that the longboats were made ready, and we thought of nothing but of going on shore to refresh ourselves after our tiring journey.

As soon as we arrived in the bay, we found it to be a very suitable place for astronomical observations, and we at once resolved to use all means to do so: for that end it was necessary to have a spacious house, carry our instruments there, and be able to use them both day and night during the short time we were to stay there. There was a difficulty in all this: Jesuits, all mathematicians, and various instruments carried on shore might offend the feelings of a Dutch commander in a fairly new colony, and make him suspect something other than what we gave out. We were even advised to disguise ourselves, and not to appear to be Jesuits; but we did not think it fit, and we found by what followed that our dress caused us no problems at all.

After we had considered the matter, it was resolved that Fr de Fontaney[6] and I should go visit the commissioner-general and the governor of the stronghold before the others went ashore, and that if in our conversation we found it possible to broach the subject of making observations, we would do so. We went straight to the fort then, without any other recommendation. The sentinel stopped us at the first gate, according to the custom of garrisons, until an officer of the guard came, and having learnt that we had come to pay a visit to the commissioner-general and the governor, he commanded us to be let in, and gave us a soldier to conduct us to their apartment.

Their residence consists of a large building, two storeys high, and very solidly constructed. It is topped by a fine terrace paved with broad flagstones, with balconies and iron railings all round; they usually go there to take the fresh air. This country has so temperate a climate that it is never very cold there, except when a south wind blows; and though it was the middle of winter then, it was so hot in the daytime that they were glad to go and take the fresh air in the evening.

We went first into a great hall where they preach every Sunday until the Protestant church is finished that is being built outside the fort. On both sides of that hall there are quite handsome apartments; we were shown into that on the left, where we were received by Mr van der Stel, and where soon afterwards Baron van Reede came to see us. He is a man of quality, about fifty years of age, handsome, civil, wise, and learned, and thinks and speaks well on all subjects; we were extremely surprised to meet with so much politeness at the Cape of Good Hope, and much more so at the civilities and many signs of friendship which we received at that first interview. Fr de Fontaney, whose interpreter I was at that time in Portuguese, finding such fortunate dispositions for our design, told the commissioner-general that there were in all six Jesuits who were bound for the Indies and China,

---

6. Fr Jean de Fontaney (1643–1710) was the superior of the six Jesuits going to China on the *Oiseau* in 1685.

and that, not being at all accustomed to the fatigues of the sea, we needed to take a little air on land to recover from so long a voyage; that we dared not do so before we knew their views, whether this would please them. The commissioner-general did not allow me to interpret all that Fr de Fontaney had said, but soon interrupting me, said in Portuguese, "You will do us the greatest pleasure in the world, Fathers, to come and refresh yourselves on land; we will contribute all that we can to aid your recovery."

This answer was so favourable that we went a little further; we told him that, once on shore, we should be glad to employ ourselves for the public good, and then to communicate to him our observations; and in this way to acknowledge to some degree the civilities that he had shown us. We said we had brought with us from France several mathematical instruments, amongst which there were some very appropriate for finding out the true longitude of countries through which we passed, without any need of the eclipses of the sun and moon; we explained to him the new way of observing by the satellites of Jupiter, for which the learned Mr Cassini[7] had made such good tables. I added that in this way we would render a considerable service to their pilots, by giving them the sure longitude for the Cape of Good Hope, which they only knew by guessing, a very doubtful way that many times deceived them, and very considerably too. He told us that we would oblige him in doing this, and that seeing we wanted to work at that discovery, he offered us a very suitable place for observing. At the same time he ordered a summer house in the Company's garden to be made ready for us to lodge in while the ambassador remained in the roads.

We replied that the civility which he showed us would not stop there, and that we hoped our ambassador would have the goodness to thank him and profit by this discovery. Then we showed him our patents for being the king's mathematicians, which we

7. Jean-Dominique Cassini (1625–1712), born in county of Nice, became the first director of the new observatory in Paris.

had already spoken about. "You increase my joy, Fathers," replied the commissioner, "in letting me see that I comply with the will and orders of so great a king, for whom I shall entertain a profound respect as long as I live. However, I am not vexed that you did not speak to me of that before I obliged you to accept a lodging, which I offered you with all my heart." They brought us tea, as it is the custom among the people of the East Indies, and after quite a long discussion about different matters, we took leave of these gentlemen, and withdrew. The commander followed us to conduct us to the apartment that was offered us in the Company's great garden.

We were greatly surprised to find one of the loveliest and most curious gardens that ever I saw in a country that looks like one of the most dismal and sterile places in the world. It lies above the houses between the town and Table Mountain, and on the side of the fort, from which it is about 200 yards distant. It is 1,411 yards in length and 235 in breadth. The beauty of it consists not as in France, in compartments, beds of flowers, or fountains. They could have them if the Dutch [East India] Company wished to pay for them, for a lively stream coming from the mountain runs through the garden. But there you have walks reaching out of sight, planted with lemon, pomegranate, and orange trees, which are protected from the wind by thick high hedges, formed of a kind of laurel, which they call *spek*, always green and quite similar to the *filaria*. By the layout of the walks, this garden is divided into several indifferent squares, some of which are full of fruit trees, including, besides apple, pear, quince, apricot trees and the excellent fruits of Europe, in addition pineapples, banana trees, and several others that bear the rarest fruits to be found in the several parts of the world which have been transported here, where they are most carefully cultivated. The other squares are sown with roots, pulses, and herbs, and some with the most esteemed flowers of Europe, and others that we have never seen before, which are particularly fragrant and beautiful. The gentlemen of the [Dutch East] India Company, to whom it belongs, as we have already said, have caused it to be made, that they may always have in that place a kind of store of all sorts of victuals for their ships that go to, or come from, the Indies, which never fail to stop at the Cape of Good Hope.

The ships that come from the Indies arrive there in the beginning of March, either alone or several together, and there they wait for the fleet from Europe, which comes in April. By that means they have news, whether or not they are at war, and set out all together, so that by the great number and strength of their ships, they may be in a position not to fear attacks from pirates or their enemies.

There is a great building at the entrance to the garden, where the Company's slaves live, numbering, so it is said, five hundred. Some of them are employed in cultivating the garden, and the rest in other necessary labour. About the middle of the wall, on the side looking towards the fort, there is a small pavilion where nobody lives. Its lower storey consists of a vestibule open to the garden and the fort, with two rooms on each side; over that there is a room open on all sides, between two terraces paved with brick, and surrounded by balustrades; one faces north, the other south. This pavilion seemed to be specially made for our purposes, for on the one side we looked wide open to the north, the view of which was absolutely necessary to us, because it is like the south in relation to our country. Whilst they were preparing that pavilion, which with the Dutch I shall call our observatory, we went on board to give the ambassador and our Fathers an account of all that had passed.

The next day the commissioner and commander sent us on board all sorts of refreshments. The officer who was ordered to present these to the ambassador on their behalf told us that these gentlemen had also sent us a boat to carry us and our instruments ashore. Having during the night prepared those which we thought we might need, we put them into the boat, and so went to the observatory on [Saturday] 2nd June 1685 . . .

Monday after dinner we went to the fort to see the gentlemen, and communicate to them the observations which we had already made, and those that we were going to make that evening to decide the true longitude of the Cape. On our return all these gentlemen decided to accompany us, to witness this observation. We went together to the terrace to show them our instruments, which seemed very fine and curious to them, when we saw our ambassador, who had come *incognito* the day before to walk in the garden and found it so pleasant that he returned again the next day to walk along its paths with most of the officers of both ships and the gentlemen in his retinue. The ambassador and commissioner had exchanged many civilities from the very day of our arrival, and no day passed without sending one another presents. Mr van Reede, seeing him, immediately came down from the terrace where he was observing the skies with us, and after one or two turns, meeting the ambassador as by chance, they conversed with each other to their mutual satisfaction.

When the ambassador had gone, the commissioner, with Messers de Saint-Martin, van der Stel, and Bocheros, stayed with us in the observatory till ten o'clock at night . . . The following day, Tuesday, 5 June, at ten o'clock, the gentlemen returned to the observatory and stayed there until two in the afternoon to see us calculate the height and distance of Table Mountain, and to look at our instruments . . .

The Abbé de Choisy wished to witness our observations, and for a time took part in our activities.

Towards the evening we received notice sent from our ship that we must come on board early next morning; all six of us went immediately to the fort to take leave of the Dutch gentlemen, and give them our thanks; for indeed we could not be more civilly nor more kindly treated than we had been. Furthermore, when we went on board we found presents of tea and Canary wine which the governor sent us, in thanks for a microscope and a small burning glass we had given him.

These gentlemen seemed all much affected at our departure. "We pray to God," said they, embracing us tenderly, "that the design for which you are going to China may succeed, and that you may bring a great number of infidels to the knowledge of the

Ok-muen Pipith Raja (ออกหมื่นพิพิธราชา), *Siamese* khunnang, *who went in 1688 with the mission to Pope Innocent XI and Louis XIV, drawn by Carlo Maratta (BAV, Vat. Lat. 14166)*

true God." At length we parted, very much touched ourselves by their good wishes and civilities. Passing near the governor's chambers, we were shown in a tub full of water two little fish, no longer than one's finger. The Portuguese call one of them gold-fish, and the other silverfish, because, in truth, the tail of the male seems to be golden, and the female's silver. We were told that these fish came from China, and that the persons of quality in these countries as well as the Japanese greatly esteemed them, and kept them in their houses as a curiosity. We saw some of them afterwards in the palace of the governor-general of Batavia, and at Siam in the palace of my lord Constance,[8] minister of that kingdom, and of some Chinese mandarins. The ambassador had requested Mr van Reede to write to the governor-general of Batavia for him to give us a pilot to conduct us to Siam. The commissioner-general agreed to this with pleasure, and sent the ambassador next day a very obliging letter for that governor, in which towards the end he added, without any solicitation from us, a word in our favour. We spent the night packing up our instruments again, and next morning before dawn we put them into a longboat which the commander had ordered to be in readiness for us, and so we went on board again.

This is all that happened at the Cape of Good Hope in relation to our observations. Though we worked hard at them day and night they were not the only things we did. No sooner had we got possession of our little observatory than the Catholics in that colony, who are pretty numerous, heard about it, and were very pleased. In the mornings and evenings they came secretly to us. They came from all countries, and were of all conditions, free men, slaves, French, Germans, Portuguese, Spaniards, Flemings, and Indians. Those who could not otherwise express themselves,

8. The 1688 English translation of Tachard had "the Lord Constance" and the 1686 French original, "Seigneur Constance". Phaulkon received his Siamese title, Ok-ya Wichayen, about 1683, and was made a French count by Louis XIV in 1687. The rather inflated English and French titles were undoubtedly justified on the grounds Phaulkon was considered a minister of state.

because we did not understand their language, fell on their knees and kissed our hands. They pulled rosaries and medals out of their bosoms to shows that they were Catholics, they wept and struck their chests. This language of the heart, so much more touching than words, affected us deeply, and obliged us to embrace those poor people which Christian charity made us look upon as our brothers. We comforted them as best we could, exhorting them to persevere in the faith of Jesus Christ, humbly and faithfully to serve their masters, and to bear their troubles with patience. We commended them particularly to examine their consciences at night and honour the Holy Virgin, who was best able to procure them more grace to live like Christians and to keep them from heresy. Those who spoke French, Latin, Spanish, or Portuguese were confessed. We visited the sick in their houses and in the hospital. This was all that could be done for their consolation in so short a time, as they were not free to come on board our ship and hear mass, and we were not permitted to say it to them on shore. Nevertheless it must have been suspected at the Cape that we carried them the sacrament, for two of our Fathers returning one day from the ship with a microscope in their hands covered with gilt leather, two or three of the inhabitants walking on the shore imagined it to be the Holy Sacrament which they were carrying to Catholics in a box. They drew near to the Father to know the truth of the matter; the Father told them what it was, and to convince them, made them look into the microscope. Then one of them said to him, "Sir, I thought it might have been so, because I know that you are the greatest enemies of our religion." We could not help smiling at that remark, but without replying we continued on our way straight to the fort.

It only remains for me in what concerns the Cape of Good Hope to relate what we learnt of the state of the country. For some of our Fathers were charged to make enquiries about that, whilst the others were taken up with their observations. With that in mind we tried to obtain from Mr van der Stel, in the several conversations we had with him, all that could contribute to our information, and we made the acquaintance of a young physician from Breslau in Silesia, called Mr Claudius, whom the Dutch retain at the Cape because of his considerable capacity. Seeing that he had already travelled in China and Japan, where he became accustomed to observing everything, and that he draws and paints animals and plants very well, the Dutchmen kept him to assist them in their discoveries of new lands, and work at a natural history of Africa. He has already completed two large in-folio volumes about various plants, drawn lifelike, and has pasted a collection of the plants he has onto the leaves of another volume. Without doubt Mr van Reede, who always kept these books at home, and who showed them to us, proposes to present to the public a *Hortus Africus* following his *Hortus Malabaricus*. If these books had been for sale, we would have spared no cost to buy them and send them to the king's library. Since this learned doctor has already travelled some 120 leagues to the north and east of the country to make new discoveries, it is from him that we obtained all the knowledge we have of the place, of which he gave us a small map which he had drawn, together with some drawings of the inhabitants of the country, and of the rarest animals, which are included here. The most remarkable things we learnt are recorded below.

The Dutch, finding that an establishment in that place would be convenient for the ships which they send each year to the Indies, made a treaty with the most important chiefs of the people there, who consented for a certain quantity of tobacco and brandy to surrender that country to them, and to move further inland. This agreement was made about the year 1653,[9] and since that time they have worked hard to establish a solid colony at the Cape. They now have there a large settlement and a fort with five bastions which commands all the roads. The air is very good, the soil excellent, and corn grows there as well as in Europe; they have planted vines which yield a most delicate wine.

Game is everywhere in abundance. Our officers returned from hunting with roe deer, gazelles, pheasants, and a large number of

9. It was actually 1652.

partridges as big as French grouse, and there are four sorts of them. The oxen and sheep are obtained further away among the savages of the country; this is a trade which the company reserves for itself, which buys them for a little tobacco, and then sells them again to the inhabitants of the Cape, and to foreigners who put in there for provisions. We saw sheep there that weighed eighty pounds, and had very good taste.

They also have civet cats there, many wild cats, lions, and tigers which have very fine skins; above all they have huge apes that sometimes come in troupes down from Table Mountain into the gardens of private individuals, and carry away their melons and other fruit. Nine or ten leagues from the Cape to the east there is a chain of mountains full of lions, elephants, and rhinoceros of enormous size. People whom one can trust who have travelled there assured me that they had found the footprint of an elephant two and a half feet in diameter, and that they have seen several rhinoceros* as big and tall as an average elephant. All that I can say about that is that I have seen the two horns which the animal has on its nose, joined naturally together, and so big and heavy that I was inclined to believe what I was told. The lieutenant at the fort who went on that expedition told me that the rhinoceros when enraged digs his larger horn into the ground and continues to run a kind of furrow with it, till he comes up to the person who has attacked him. The skin of this animal is so hard that it is musket-proof, unless one takes one's time to hit it when it shows its flank, the only place in its body where firearms or halberds that travellers carry can wound it. There are horses and asses of extraordinary beauty. The former have a very small head, and quite long ears. They are covered all over with black and white stripes reaching from top to bottom, about four fingers broad, and are very pretty to see.** I saw the skin of one that had been killed, which our ambassador bought to take back to France as a very curious thing. As for the asses, they are of all colours, with a

* See p. 30.
**See p. 20.

long blue streak on their backs that stretches from head to tail, and the rest of their body is like a horse, full of quite broad streaks, blue, yellow, green, black, and white, and all very lively.

Stags* are so plentiful there that they are seen in flocks like sheep, and I heard the commander's secretary say, and the commander himself too, that they had seen up to ten thousand of them together in an open space which they found in the forests. There are not so many tigers or lions as stags, but there are still a great many of them, and I can easily believe it because of the vast number of skins of those animals which they trade at the Cape. They do not keep close to the woods, but sometimes come to inhabited places, when they attack anything they meet, even men. An example of this occurred when we were there, and the commissioner-general told us about it. Two men walking at some distance from the houses saw a tiger, one fired at it and missed it, and it immediately fell on him and brought him to the ground; the other, seeing in what great danger his companion was, fired at the tiger, but only wounded his friend in the thigh; the tiger in the meantime, having not been hurt, left his prey, and chased after the man who fired. The first one got up again and came in time to assist his friend and kill the tiger. They say that these animals have such an instinct that among a hundred men they will single out the person who has fired at them, and leave all the others to attack just this one. A month before, a very similar accident occurred with a lion who tore to pieces a man and his servant, quite close to the houses, and was afterwards killed.

At the Cape we caught a great many excellent fish. Amongst others were mullets, and the fish known in France as gilt-head bream, which are very different from real dolphins, which are much bigger, and better deserving their name because of their yellowish colour and golden specks, that make them seem like one of the loveliest fish that swims in the sea. We also took great numbers of soles and some crampfish. The crampfish or ray is an

* See p. 36.

ugly beast, very soft, which, when you catch it numbs you in the hand and arm. We saw many seals there, which looked like wolves. There are also penguins there too. These are waterfowl, without wings, and almost all the time in the water, being truly amphibious.

In the year 1681, Mr van der Stel settled a new colony, consisting of eighty-two families, nine or ten leagues further inland, and called the place Hollenbok. Some maintain that there are gold mines on the Cape. They showed us stones found there which seemed to confirm that opinion; for they are heavy, and with a microscope one can see that there are on all sides small particles that look like gold.

But the most curious thing we found at the Cape was an exact map of the places newly discovered by the Dutch, with an account in Latin of the different peoples that inhabit them. Both were given to us by a reliable person who only wrote down what he himself had seen, and an exact translation of which follows.

"The southern point of Africa is no less remote from Europe than the habits of its inhabitants are different from ours. For these people are ignorant of the creation of the world, the redemption of man, and the mystery of the most Holy Trinity. However, they adore a God, but the knowledge they have of Him is very confused. In honour of Him they kill cows and lambs and offer Him the flesh and milk in sacrifice, as a token of their gratitude towards that divinity, who grants them, so they believe, sometimes rain and sometimes fair weather according to their needs. They expect no other life after this. With all that, they have still some good qualities which should restrain us from despising them; for they have more charity and fidelity one toward another than is to be found commonly amongst Christians. Adultery and theft are with them capital crimes, always punished by death. Though every man has the liberty to take as many wives as he is able to maintain, yet none of them, even among the richest, is to be found with more than three.

"These people are divided into several nations, who have all the same way of living. Their ordinary food is milk and the meat of the cattle which they keep in great quantity. Each of these nations has their head or captain whom they obey; that office is hereditary, and goes from father to son. The right of succession belongs to the eldest, and to retain their authority and respect, they are the only heirs of their fathers, the younger having no other inheritance but the obligation of serving their elders. Their clothes are just plain sheepskins with the wool, prepared with cows' dung and a certain grease that renders them insupportable both to the eye and smell. The first nation in the language of the country is called Sonquas. The Europeans call those people Hottentots, perhaps because they have always that word in their mouth when they meet strangers. As they are very nimble, strong, bold, and more expert than others in handling their arms, which are the javelin and arrows, they go and serve other nations as soldiers, and so there is not one nation who besides their own natives do not also have Sonquas among their warriers. In their own country they live in deep caves, and sometimes in houses like other people. They live mostly by hunting, at which they are very skilled: they kill elephants, rhinoceros, elks, stags, gazelles, roe deer, and several other animals, of which there is a prodigious quantity on the Cape; they also gather at certain times the honey which the bees make in hollows in trees and rocks."

I shall interrupt this account for a moment to relate what we ourselves have seen of these people or what we learned about them from reliable persons. The Hottentots, being persuaded that there is no other life after this, work as little as possible and take things as easily as they can in this world. To hear them talk even when they are serving the Dutch for a little bread, tobacco, or brandy, they consider those who till the land of their country as slaves, and as people with no courage who shut themselves up inside houses and forts to be secure from their enemies; whereas their people live safely in the open fields without stooping so low as to till the land. By that way of living they pretend to demonstrate that they are masters of the earth, and the happiest people in the world, because they alone live in liberty and at ease, in what consists their contentment. Whilst we were in the

Ok-khun Wiset Puban (ออกขุนวิเศษภูบาล), *Siamese* khunnang, *who went in 1688 with the mission to Pope Innocent XI and Louis XIV, drawn by Carlo Maratta (BAV, Vat. Lat. 14166)*

Company's garden, a leading man among them, seeing how civilly we were treated by the leaders of the Dutch there, came to the observatory, and there meeting Fr de Fontaney, presented him with two oranges, saying to him in Portuguese "Reverendo Padre, géral dos Ottentots a vossa Senhoria," thereby intimating that his captain and nation congratulated us on our arrival.

Whatever good opinion they may have of themselves, they lead a wretched life. They are excessively dirty, and it would seem that they try to make themselves hideous. When they wish to dress up, they rub their heads, face, and hands with soot from their kettles, and when that is lacking they use a certain kind of black grease that makes them stink and look so horrid that they cannot be endured. Their hair, which is naturally almost as woolly as the hair of negroes, forms little round knots with this grease, to which they fasten pieces of copper or glass. The most important among them add to these ornaments large ivory rings which they wear on their arms above and below the elbows. Their food is far more surprising, for they make a delicious dish of the vermin that breed in the skins they wear. We have seen this more than once, otherwise we could never have believed it. The women, in addition to this dress, wrap animals' guts or small skins around their legs; they do this to stop their legs being scratched by thorns when they go gathering food in the woods, and always have some food at hand should they feel hungry. Their ornament consists of several strings of beads made of shells or bones of different colours which they make into necklaces or belts, and some thick rings which they wear on their arms.

However, barbarity has not completely effaced all traces of humanity in those people, and there still remains some residue of virtue; they are trustworthy, and the Dutch allow them free access to their houses without fear of being robbed by them. Nevertheless it is said that they are not so reserved to strangers, or to the Dutch who are newcomers, who do not know them so well as to get them punished. They are generous and helpful, and keep nothing wholly to themselves. When they have anything given to them, if it can be divided, they give a share of it to the first of their people they meet, and will even look around for someone for that purpose, and usually keep the smallest share of what they have for themselves.

When one of them is convicted of a capital crime among themselves, such as theft or adultery, the captain and chiefs assemble, and after having fairly tried the prisoner, they carry out their own sentence; they kill him by beating him with sticks, everyone coming in rank order to give him a blow, after the captain has given him the first one; or they run him through with their javelins. They say they are astrologers and herbalists, and men whose word can be trusted assured us that they understood quite well the disposition of the sky, and that they could distinguish natural remedies, even at night, by their touch and smell. They are extremely jealous of their liberty, and the [Dutch] commander told us that he had wanted to tame one of them by making him his domestic servant in his youth. However, when he grew up, he had to be allowed to leave, something he insisted on, saying that he could not submit to the constraint of a regular life, that the Dutch and other such nations were slaves of the earth, and that the Hottentots were the masters of it, that they were not forced to stand with their hats continually under their arms, and to observe a hundred inconvenient customs; they ate when they were hungry, and followed no other rules than what nature taught them; in short, they are happy, sprightly, brusque in their words, and seem to have wit.

They have some very odd customs. When a woman has lost her first husband, she ought to cut off as many joints of her fingers, beginning with the little finger, as she marries new husbands. The men in their youth make themselves half-eunuchs, pretending that this contributes greatly to the preservation and increase of their agility. They are all either hunters or shepherds; the former live in caves and live off their prey. The latter feed on their flocks and their milk; they live in huts made of branches of trees, covered with skins and mats like tents. The door of these huts is so low that you have to crawl to enter them, and the roof so low too that you cannot stand upright in them. Four of five families live in one of these hovels which are not bigger than five or six paces in circumference. They make a fire in the middle, and the family quarters are only distinguished by holes dug in the ground two feet deep. But let us now continue with the account which we interrupted.

"The second nation is that of the Namaquas, the sketch of whom is shown here.* The first time we discovered them was in 1682. We entered their village, and through some Kaffirs who served us as guides, we sent their captain tobacco, a pipe, brandy, a knife, and some bits of coral. The captain accepted our presents, and in gratitude sent us two fat sheep, each of whose tails weighed more than twenty pounds, with a great vessel full of milk, and a certain herb which they call *kanna*; it is probably that famous plant which the Chinese name ginseng, for Mr Claudius who has seen it at China, affirms that he found two plants of it upon the Cape, and showed us the complete illustration of it which he had drawn to the life, and which Mr Thevenot[10] lately gave me a sight of, in the same way as can be seen in the illustration of the Sonquas. They use *kanna* as frequently as the Indians use betel and areca. Next day one of their captains came to us. He was a man whose great height and particularly proud look were respected by his fellows. He brought along with him fifty young men, and as many women and girls. Each of the men carried a flute in their hands made of a certain reed very well fashioned which produced a quite pleasant sound. The captain having given the sign, they then all played on these instruments together. The women and girls mingled their voices to the music, and made a noise by clapping hands. These two groups were lined up in two rings one within another, the first, which was on the outside, and made up of the men, surrounded the other ring of the women on the inside; they danced in circles, the men turning to the right and the women to the left, whilst an old man

* See p. 60.

10. Melchisédech Thevenot was the author of four volumes, *Relations de divers voyages curieux* . . . Paris, 1663–1672, illustrated by many maps.

standing in the middle with a stick in his hand beat the time and regulated their cadence. Their music at a distance seemed to be pleasant, and even harmonious, but there was no kind of regularity in their dance, or rather it was a mere confusion. The Namaquas are held in great reputation among those people and are accounted brave, warlike, and potent, though their greatest forces do not exceed two thousand men under arms. They are all tall and strong, have good natural sense; and when any question is put to them, they weigh their words well before they answer, and all their answers are short and grave. They seldom laugh, and speak very little, the women seem to be crafty, and are nowhere near so grave as the men.

"The third nation are the Ubiquas. They are professional robbers, and rob Africans as well as strangers. Though they are not able to send five hundred men into the field, it is not easy to root them out, because they retreat into inaccessible mountains. The Gouriquas make the fourth nation which is not very numerous. The Ilassiquas makes the fifth, and are more numerous; they are rich and powerful, little versed in the art of war; contrary to the sixth nation, I mean the Gouriquas,[11] who are great warriors. The seventh nation are the Sousiquas, and the Odiquas are their allies."

In the great rivers there is a huge creature which they call a sea cow, and equals the rhinoceros in size; its flesh, or rather its lard, is good to eat, and has a very pleasant taste. I have provided an illustration of it here.* As for trees, plants and flowers, there are infinite numbers of them, and some very curious not only for their beauty, but also for their special attributes.

In the journey they made, which lasted five whole months, they advanced as far north as the Tropic [of Capricorn]; that is to say they discovered two hundred leagues of the country, always keeping within ten or twelve leagues of the Western Ocean [the South Atlantic]. The commander Mr van der Stel was there in

11. *Sic.* Possibly Odiquas is meant.
* See p. 44.

person, accompanied by fifty-eight well-armed men. His carriage came after him and forty wagons with 28 horses, 300 sheep, and 150 oxen. These last carried the baggage and pulled the wagons, and the sheep served as food to the travellers. He set out with his company from the Cape of Good Hope about the end of May, which is the wintertime in that country, and he chose that season so that he might not lack water and forage in the deserts which he had to cross. They discovered some different nations, at the 28th degree latitude, who live in a pleasant country abounding in all sorts of fruit and animals. Before they arrived there, they found many deserts and mountains, one of which was so high that the commander assured us they were forty days in reaching its peak. They thought they would all die of thirst, together with their animals, and were many times in danger of being devoured by the wild beasts which they met in herds. The commander had much trouble in saving himself from a rhinoceros of enormous size that was within three steps of him, ready to tear him to pieces, had he not escaped it by flinging himself to one side, and getting out of the animal's sight, which looked around for him for a long while to rip him asunder.

But when they came to the 27th degree latitude, about ten or twelve leagues from the ocean's coasts, they met a very numerous tribe, far more tractable than any they had met before. Mr van der Stel had with him two trumpeters, some oboists, and five or six violinists, and as soon as the people heard the sound of these instruments, they came flocking around them, and sent for their musicians, consisting of nearly thirty persons, who almost all had different instruments. The person in the middle had a very long cornet made of the gut of a bullock dried and prepared, the rest had flageolets and flutes made of canes of different lengths and thicknesses. They played their instruments in much the same way as we do ours, but with the difference that there was only one hole, which reached from one end to the other, and is much wider than that of the flutes and flageolets commonly used in France. To tune them, they made use of a ring that has a small opening in the middle, which they move up or down in the pipe by means of a little stick, according to the note they want to have it tuned to. They hold their instrument with one hand, and with the other press their lips against it so that they can blow fully into the pipe. Their music is simple, but harmonious. The head of the band after making all the other musicians tune their instruments according to the key and note of the cornet, which he plays, selects the tune that is to be played, and with a great stick beats the time so that he can be seen by everyone.

The music is always accompanied by dances, which consist in leaping, and certain foot movements, without shifting from the place they are in. The women and girls make a big ring around the dancers, but only clap their hands, and sometimes beat their feet with the rhythm. Only the players of the instruments can change their place when dancing, with the exception of the conductor, who stands without moving so that he can keep the tune and the rhythm.

The men are shapely and strong; they have long hair, which they allow to hang down to their shoulders. They bear arrows and javelins, which look rather like lances. Their clothes consist of a long cloak made from a tiger's skin, which reaches down to their heels. Some of them are as white as Europeans, but they cover themselves with grease and the powder of a certain black stone, in which they rub over their face and their whole body. Seeing their fields and woods abound with very rare remedies of all kinds, they are all herbalists. Many of them are very skilful in minerals too, which they know how to melt and prepare, but they have no great esteem for them, perhaps because there are a great many gold, silver, and copper mines in their country. Their women naturally are very fair, but to please their husbands they make themselves as black as them.

Married women have the top part of their heads shaved, and wear big pointed shells on their ears. They cover themselves with tigers' skins, which they tie around their bodies with thongs. These people greatly value a certain stone core, which is only found in the centre of some rocks, and is quite hard and very dark in colour. Experience has taught them that this mineral has a wonderful property of causing birth when they are in labour, and makes their cows, sheep, and goats easily give birth. When the Dutch blew up a great rock with a mine, in which a lot of this was found, they showed their displeasure and complained as if they had been robbed of a great treasure. Upon my return [to the Cape from Siam] I had a piece of that mineral given me, with some others which had been found in that land.

Many other sorts of animals and insects are to be found there, and they are illustrated here. The first is a horned viper, called the cerastes, which has not been discovered before and whose poison is extremely dangerous. Secondly, there is a chamelion that can change into any colour it wants, and has a cry like a rat. Thirdly there is a lizard, which when one hits it makes a sound like a child crying, and when angry raises all the scales on its body which is covered with them. Its tongue is bluish and very long, and when anybody comes near it, it can be heard snorting very violently. There is another lizard found there, marked with three white crosses, but its bite is not so dangerous as the first.*

From all that has been said, it is quite clear that this part of Africa is no less peopled, no less rich, and no less fertile in all kinds of fruits and animals, than the other parts which have already been discovered, though it has been so long neglected. The people who inhabit it are neither cruel nor wild, and lack neither docility nor wit. This is best seen each day by the trade which the Dutch conduct with them. But it is their great misfortune, and cannot be lamented enough, that being so numerous a people, they have no knowledge of the true God, and that nobody tries to instruct them. People travel all over their country, and even visit them in their dwellings in the thickest forests, they cross over their scorching deserts, and with much hardship, toil, and danger, climb over their steepest mountains. But this is only done to discover their mines, to examine the fecundity of their lands, to learn their secrets, and the virtues of their traditional remedies, and to grow rich by trad-

* See pp. 50 and 54.

ing with them. The truth is that such an enterprise, and the execution of so great and difficult a design, would be very laudable, if zeal for the salvation of their souls were included in some degree, and if in trading with them, they were taught the way to heaven and the eternal truths.

Zealous missionaries would be very necessary in that remote part of Africa. They would look upon these people as ransomed by the blood of Jesus Christ, and for all they are savages, they are as capable of glorifying God to all eternity as the nations which are most polite. In the first instance, the missionaries would minister to the Catholics of the Cape, who for want of priests have been many years without masses and the sacraments. They would at the same time instruct the Hottentots who are already known, and the easier to be won over to Jesus Christ, in that they have no considerable vice that may divert them from Christianity. In the process of time they might advance to the most distant peoples, of whom, by God's grace, many might be brought to the sheepfold of our Saviour.

These are the particulars concerning the Cape which we learned during our stay there . . .

The following day, 13th March [1686], the wind abated, and we came to anchor in the bay, among seven great Dutch ships that made up the East India fleet that was to return to Europe as soon as three or four more ships, which they expected any day, came to the Cape. The ambassador sent a compliment to the governor of the fort, who received it no less well than the time before when we passed there. We saluted the fort with seven guns, and they returned our salute gun for gun. While we were taking in water and other necessary provisions, I went to pay a visit to the governor, who had asked for news of the six Jesuits who he had seen the year before. He made me many kind offers, proposing a friend's house if I would like to stay on shore, because the observatory had been pulled down for a grander one to be built and was not yet finished. Being informed that I was to return to the Indies with several other Jesuits, he added very obligingly that all should be ready on our arrival, and invited me and all my companions beforehand to come and refresh ourselves there. After all these civilities, he gave me as a present four fine tigers' skins, and a little tame beast which he had taken on his last expedition; from its hair and size, it resembles a squirrel, and had almost the shape of one; when he gave it to me, he gave me to understand it was the implacable enemy of snakes, and waged a vicious war with them.

It was then well into the time for gathering grapes, and we ate African grapes which are plentiful, and have a specially good taste. Their white wine is very delicate, and if the Dutch knew as well how to cultivate vines as to make colonies and pursue trade, they would have excellent wines of the other colour.

The governor told me that he had just returned from a great journey he had made up into the country to the north, where he had discovered many peoples, who have some form of government, and a well-ordered administration, as may be seen in the description of the Cape of Good Hope [above].

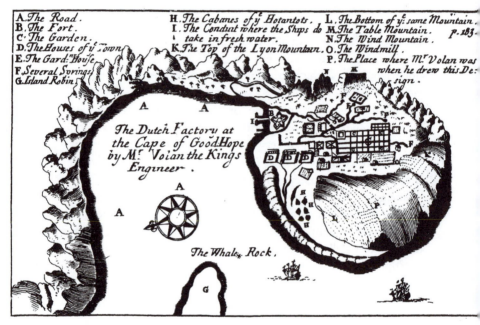

A. The Road.
B. The Fort.
C. The Garden.
D. The Houses of ye Town
E. The Gard:n House
F. Several Springs
G. Island Robin

H. The Cabanes of ye Hotantots.
I. The Condut where the Ships do take in fresh water.
K. The Top of the Lyon Mountain.

L. The Bottom of ye same Mountain. p. 183.
M. The Table Mountain.
N. The Wind Mountain.
O. The Windmill.
P. The Place where Mr Volan was when he drew this Design.

The Dutch Factory at the Cape of Good Hope by Mr Voian the Kings Engineer.

The Whale Rock.

The Dutch factory at the Cape

SIMON DE LA LOUBÈRE

The Kingdom of Siam, Book II, pp. 482–487 of the 1987 French edition, following the first edition of 1691; Tome II, pp. 183–186 of the 1693 English edition. Translated from the French original by Michael Smithies.

I am giving here three different views [of the Cape], two of which are entirely new, and the third is that seen from the roads, copied from a very good Dutch map.*

Everyone knows that the Dutch have an important establishment there which supports their shipping in the East Indies. The fort which defends it would not count for much in Europe, but suffices in a country where there are no neighbours to be feared, and where any enemies would have to come from a long way off, and consequently with great difficulty.

The [Dutch] Company's garden, the plan of which is found in one of these prints, is very spacious, as can be judged when comparing it to the fort. And, although the soil is not excellent, it provides in abundance cabbages, pumpkins, oranges, and, in a word, the vegetables and fruits which do not spoil at sea, and which seafaring men greatly desire during long voyages.

I observed in one spot, behind the same protective screen, a camphor tree, a European fig, and a shrub some two feet high which was said to be that which bears tea [leaves], and which I

---

* See pp. 66 and 108.

would have taken for a small pear tree. It had neither flowers nor fruits, and very few leaves. Immediately after, protected by another screen, were two or three pineapple plants, and that was all that I was shown which was rare for that place. Grapes are not less well known, but there are only those which the Dutch have planted. The wine is white and quite good. Some of our party went to the top of Table Mountain to look for rare plants, but found none. After looking closely for them, there was none that was special which other plants of those lands do not have. The shells found there are not the result of the Flood, as some had supposed: birds, monkeys, and Hottentots have transported them and left them there.

The walks in the garden almost look after themselves, because the soil only produces moss if it is not cultivated. Moreover the neatness of the garden neither reveals careful husbandry nor indicates too great a negligence, like merchants' kitchen gardens, more concerned with the profit they can extract from them than with pleasures they will not enjoy.

The water which feeds it through several small channels enters the garden after a race from a mill which it turns, and below the garden serves for laundering. Only a part is diverted into a reservoir on the shores of the roads where the ships come to take on their provision.

The garden is divided into several squares, about as big as a quarter of the Place Royale.[1] They are surrounded by hedges to protect them from the winds which are sometimes strong enough to sink vessels in the roads if they do not have good anchors and strong cables. These winds are formed from the clouds which sometimes pile up between Table Mountain and that called Wind Mountain and which cause these storms. A walk of lemon and orange trees, planted in the soil, goes from one end of the garden to the other, and feels the full effects of their fury. Apart from that, the location of the garden, and that of the village a little closer to the roads, are very good, for they are very well placed

1. The Place Royale is now the Place des Vosges in Paris.

to catch the sun, and protected from the southern winds which are very cold in those lands. The Dutch, who are used to them, say that if the wind from the southwest does not blow during their summer, which is our winter, sicknesses of the lungs are frequent and dangerous.

The short time I stayed there did not permit me to learn much of the habits of the Hottentots, the indigenous people of the Cape, although the extreme simplicity in which they live would not make for extensive study. They are called Hottentots because when they dance, they only utter one word while singing—"hottentot." Their love of tobacco and brandy, which outsiders offer them, and which caused them to admit the Dutch to their country, allows them to dance as much as they wish; that is, they strike the ground with one foot, then another, like a group treading grapes, always repeating rapidly "hottenot, hottentot," but in a low voice, as if they were out of breath, or were afraid of waking someone. This mute song has no diversity of pitch, but of measure: the two first syllables of "hottentot" are always two crotchets, and the last always a semibreve.

They go completely naked, as can be seen in the accompanying illustration.* They only have a skin over their shoulders like a cloak, which they often remove; then they only have a small leather purse suspended around their neck attached by a string, and a piece of leather, a little larger than one's hand, hung in front of them, attached to another string passing round their body. But this piece does not cover them when they are seen sideways or when they make a sudden movement.

They are of good height and walk as easily as one could wish. They are born as white as Spaniards, but have very woolly hair and features ressembling those of negroes. They are always so black because they cover their bodies and faces with grease. They also put grease on their heads, and can be smelt twenty paces away when the wind comes from behind them. Our people gave them cooking pots and cauldrons to wash; before anything else,

* See p. 112.

The Hottentots of the Cape

they took the grease in handfuls and anointed their whole body with it, from head to foot. The grease protects them from the air and the sun, makes them healthy and lithe, and they prefer these natural advantages to sweet odours and charm. They are so agile that several of them can outrun horses. They swim across any river. They are clever at firing arrows and throwing javelins, and they are bold to the point of fearlessness. They sometimes confront a lion, provided they have enough skin or rags to protect their left arm. They then put it in the jaws of the animal, and strike its flank with a javelin or a knife which they hold in the right hand. If there are two of them, one kills the lion while the other teases it. If they are several and have nothing to protect them from the lion's blows, they do not expose themselves [to its fury] all at once; one of them usually dies, but the lion dies too from the blows administered by the others. Sometimes they are all saved and dispatch the lion.

Their women cover themselves in grease like the men, although they like some decoration, like attaching small bones and shells to their short woolly hair, covered in fat. They also sport necklaces of coloured glass, bones, or some other material, according to what visitors have given or sold them. They wear on each leg some fifty leather rings which beat against each other with some noise when they dance, and which protect them from the brambles when they go to gather wood, for this is their task, not that of their husbands.

Both men and woman ate entrails almost without emptying them when our men gave them some, and they hardly put them a moment over the coals. If we offered them brandy, they picked up the first shell they found on the ground, and after blowing into it, used it to drink from. They eat their lice like the Cochinchinese, and, when others find this strange, they reply that it is because their lice eat them.

They dwell in small huts made of leaves or thick woven reeds, the height of which reached hardly to the middle of my body, and it seemed to me that I would not have been able to sleep there stretched out. They make a hole in the ground under this matting and in the hole, which is about two feet deep, they make their fire, without bothering about the smoke from which their huts are never free. They live by hunting, fishing, and from the milk and meat of their herds.

In this poverty, they are always happy, ever singing and dancing, living without business or work, not interested in gold or silver except in so far as it is necessary to procure a little tobacco and brandy, a corruption which trade has introduced into their customs.

As some of them displayed their skills with the javelin in front of us, I offered them five or six packets of necklaces made of seeds and coloured glass. They all held my hand so tightly that I could not open it to distribute the necklaces, nor could I explain myself to them. I was some time in this difficulty until they saw that they should leave me alone to obtain what they sought. They like these necklaces for the women and, when we set sail, I learnt that one of our lackeys had sold them some for a crown. The little money they have, and which they are not concerned about, is their wages for sometimes serving the Dutch and other visitors who land at the Cape; but they do not seek out work with them.

They have only one wife each. Their chief sometimes has three, and adultery is punished by death among them. They kill their children when they have too many. And, as they marry those they keep at a very young age, many young girls among them can be seen who are already widows, lacking a joint in the small finger, for, when a woman loses her husband, she cuts the joint of the little finger, or the fourth finger; if she has been a widow many times all the small finger is cut off. She can all the same avoid this if she wishes; and there are some men who do not follow this custom when they lose their wives. Most of them remove one testicle to be more desirable to their wives, and then at the age of renunciation, they castrate themselves completely to deprive themselves of contact with them, and live to a healthier old age. The Dutch had raised a Hottentot child in the European fashion and sent him to Holland. Some time afterwards, they had him sent back to the Cape where he could have been useful for those of his tribe; but, as soon as he returned among his own, he stayed there and abandoned Dutch dress and customs.

They do not commit theft among themselves, nor in the Dutch houses, where they are received without precautions being taken. But, if theft does occur, it is punished by death. Nevertheless, in the bush, when they can steal in surety and hope not to be discovered, they sometimes murder in order to rob, and prove that their scorn for wealth is only their dislike of work.

The Dutch name their head man, and this person is their judge. But those who could not tolerate this dependency went to live further inland with other Kaffirs.

I was at first told that they had no notions of religion. But in the end I learnt that, though they have no priests or temples, they nevertheless on the new and full moons make public festivities which are like a cult. I suspect that they are tainted by Manichaeism,[2] because they recognize the principle of goodness, and that of evil, which they call the chief above and the chief below. The chief above, they say, is good; it is not necessary to pray to him but just let him be, and he always does good. But the chief below is wicked; one has to pray to him to prevent him causing harm. This is what they say, but it would seem from their outward conduct that they do not pray often. A Dutchman who had both wit and knowledge told me that he had discovered among the Hottentots the names of Hasdrubal and Bocchus.[3]

---

2. Manichaeism is the belief that Satan is in everlasting conflict with God.
3. Hasdrubal and Bocchus were Carthaginian and Mauritanean leaders.

Ok-khun Chamnan Chaichong (ออกขุนชำนาญใจจง), *Siamese* khunnang, *who went in 1688 with the mission to Pope Innocent XI and Louis XIV, drawn by Carlo Maratta (BAV, Vat. Lat. 14166)*

TENTATIVE CHRONOLOGY OF THE LIFE OF OK-KHUN CHAMNAN CHAICHONG

c. 1654		born ?Ayutthaya
1684	Mar	embarked at the bar of Siam for Goa on a Siamese frigate with a Portuguese captain
		"5 months" to reach Goa (?reached Goa Aug)
		"11 months" stay in Goa (?left Goa Jul 1685)
1686	27 Jan	left Goa for Lisbon
	27 Apr	shipwrecked off Cape Agulhas
		"31 days" overland to the Cape of Good Hope
	28 May	arrived close to the Dutch settlement at the Cape
		"nearly 4 months" at the Cape (?left late Sep)
	early Sep	embarked at the Cape for Batavia
	Nov	arrived Batavia
		"6 months" in Batavia (?left Batavia Apr 1687)
1687	Jun	departed Batavia for Siam
	Sep	arrived Siam
		Chamnan "not 6 months" in Siam before the French envoys arrive
	27 Sep	La Loubère and Céberet arrive at the bar of Siam

	4 Oct	Chamnan is one of two *ok-khun* to greet the French envoys
1688	3 Jan	departed with two other mandarins, Ok-khun Wiset Puban and Ok-muen Pipith Raja, accompanying Fr Tachard on the *Gaillard*
	21 Apr	at the Cape of Good Hope again
	1 May	departed Cape of Good Hope
	25 Jul	arrived Brest, travelled by sea to Rouen
	14 Sep	arrived Paris
	5 Nov	left Paris for Lyons; took litters to Cannes
	26 Nov	left Cannes on two feluccas for Villefranche
	29 Nov–	Monaco, San Remo, Savona
	2 Dec	arrived Genoa; afterwards, to Rapallo
	?7 Dec	arrived Livorno (Leghorn)
	15 Dec	departed Livorno
	20 Dec	Civitavecchia
	21 Dec	arrived Rome, coming up the Tiber
	23 Dec	audience with Pope Innocent XI
	24 Dec–	Sistine Chapel and other sights in Rome
1689	5 Jan	farewell audience with the pope
	7 Jan	left Rome for Civitavecchia
	9 Jan	left Civitavecchia for Marseilles
	?Feb	audience with Louis XIV in Versailles
	Mar	Paris
	?18 Nov	Port-Louis
	?Nov	Brest
1690	25 Feb	departed Brest on the *Gaillard*, one of six ships in the Duquesne-Guiton fleet bound for Pondichéry
	10 Mar	Ok-muen Pipith died on board
	Aug	departed Pondichéry
	Dec	arrived Balassor (Bengal)
1691		arrived in Ayutthaya via Mergui
1699	Jan	?met Tachard when he went to Ayutthaya on his final journey
?	died	

REFERENCES

ANDERSON, John. *English Intercourse with Siam in the Seventeenth Century.* London: Kegan Paul, 1890.

Breve Ragguaglio di quanto è accaduto in Roma à Sig. Mandarini venuti cô il P. Guido Tasciard della Compagnia di Giesù, inviato staordinario dal Ré di Siam dopo l'Udienza havuta da N.S. Innocenzo XI. Rome: Domenico Antonio Ercole, 1689.

CARRETTO, Rev. Fr. Vatican Papers of the XVII Century. *Journal of the Thailand Research Society [JSS]* 35/2 (1944): 173–189. Reprinted in *Selected Articles from JSS,* vol. 7, Relationship [*sic*] with Portugal, Holland, and the Vatican. (Bangkok: Siam Society, 1959) 177–193.

CATHOLIC MASS-MEDIA. *Somosorn 25 phi Thai-Vatican* [Chronicle of twenty-five years of Thai-Vatican relations]. Bangkok: Assumption Press, 1994.

CHALLE, Robert. *Journal d'un voyage fait aux Indes Orientales (1690–1691).* Paris: Mercure de France, 1979.

CHAUMONT, Chevalier de, and Abbé de CHOISY. *Aspects of the Embassy to Siam, 1685.* Introduced and in part translated by Michael Smithies. Chiang Mai: Silkworm Books, 1998.

CHOISY, Abbé François-Timoléon de. *Journal of a Voyage to Siam, 1685–1686*. Translated and introduced by Michael Smithies. Kuala Lumpur, Oxford University Press, 1993.

CRUYSSE, Dirk Van der. *Louis XIV et le Siam*. Paris: Fayard, 1992.

DONNEAU DE VIZÉ, Jean. *Mercure Galant*. Paris, 1687–1690.

————. *Voyage des Ambassadeurs de Siam en France*. Bangkok: Chalermnit, 1985.

FORBIN, Claude de. *The Siamese Memoirs of Count Claude de Forbin 1685–1688*. Introduced and edited by Michael Smithies. Chiang Mai: Silkworm Books, 1997.

HUTCHINSON, E.W. The French Foreign Mission in Siam during the XVIIth Century. *Journal of the Siam Society* 26/1 (1933): 1–71.

JACQ-HERGOUALC' H, Michel. *Etude historique et critique du livre de Simon de La Loubère, 'Du Royaume de Siam', Paris 1691*. Paris: Editions Recherche sur les Civilisations, 1987.

————. *Etude historique et critique du* Journal du Voyage de Siam de Claude Céberet, *Envoyé extraordinaire du Roi en 1687 et 1688*. Paris: L'Harmattan, 1992.

KEIJTS, Joannes. Letter from the *opperhoofd* and Council in Ayutthaya to Governor-General Camphuijs and Council [Batavia], 1 November 1687, VOC 1440 fol. 2230. The Hague: Algemeen Rijksarchief.

LA LOUBâRE, Simon de. *A New Historical Relation of the Kingdom of Siam*. London: Horne, Sanders, and Bennet, 1693.

LANIER, Lucien. *Etude Historique sur les Relations de la France et du Royaume de Siam de 1662 à 1703.* Versailles: Aubert, 1883.

LAUNAY, Adrien. *Histoire de la Mission de Siam 1662–1811.* 2 vols. Paris: Téqui, 1920.

Lettere scritta da Roma al Signor N.N. in cvi si dà notitia della Vdienza data da N.S. Innocenzo XI al Padre Gvido Tasciard della Compagnia di Giesv inviato dal Ré di Siam, et alli Signori mandarini venuti dal medemo Regno di Siam à di 23 Decembre 1688. Rome: Domenico Antonio Ercole, 1688.

MARTIN, François. *Mémoires.* 3 vols. Paris: Société de l'Histoire des Colonies Françaises, 1931–34.

PHRASADET SURENTHRATHIBODI, Ok-ya. Letter from the acting *phra klang* to Governor-General Camphuijs and Council [Batavia], 18 January 1688, VOC 1440 fol. 2509. The Hague: Algemeen Rijksarchief.

ROYAL INSTITUTE. *Chotmaihet ruang song tut Thai pai krung Rome khrang thi song nai paendin Somdech Phra Narai Maharaj* [Chronicle concerning the despatch of a second Thai Embassy to Rome during the reign of Phra Narai the Great]. Bangkok: Royal Institute, 1933. Reprinted 1967, Sakhon Nakhon.

SMITHIES, Michael. The Travels in France of the Siamese Ambassadors 1686–7. *Journal of the Siam Society* 77/2 (1989): 59–70.

———. Robert Challe and Siam. *Journal of the Siam Society* 81/1 (1993): 91–102.

———. Siamese mandarins on the Grand Tour, 1688–1690. *Journal of the Siam Society* 86/1 and 2 (1998): 107–118.

TACHARD, Guy. *Voyage de Siam des Pères Jésuites envoyés par le Roi au royaume de Siam.* Paris: Seneuze et Horthemels, 1686.

————. Relation ou Voyage du Père Tachard à Siam. Unpublished ms in the Archives Nationales Colonies, Paris, C1 24 (1688), 172r–211v.

————. *Second Voyage du Père Tachard et des Jésuites envoyés par le Roi au Royaume de Siam.* Paris: Horthemels, 1689.

————. Relation de voyage aux Indes 1690–1699. Unpublished ms in the Bibliothèque Nationale, Fr. 19030, ler cahier, p. 24.

VACHET, Bénigne. Unpublished section of his Mémoires, MEP vol. 112/2, pp. 239–240. Paris: Missions Etrangères.

VONGSURAVATANA, Raphaël. *Un Jésuite à la Cour de Siam.* Paris: France-Empire, 1992.

INDEX

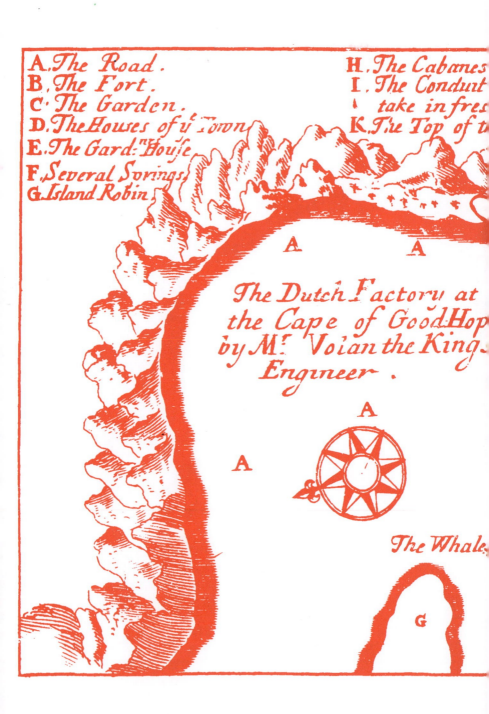

A. The Road.
B. The Fort.
C. The Garden.
D. The Houses of y.ᵉ Town.
E. The Gard:ⁿ House.
F. Several Springs.
G. Island Robin.

H. The Cabanes
I. The Conduit
  take in fres
K. The Top of t

A   A

The Dutch Factory at
the Cape of Good.Hop
by Mr. Voian the King.
Engineer.

A

A

The Whale

G